BEATITUDE SAINTS

DANIEL MORRIS-YOUNG

WIPF & STOCK · Eugene, Oregon

Wipf and Stock Publishers
199 W 8th Ave, Suite 3
Eugene, OR 97401

Beatitude Saints
By Morris-Young, Daniel
Copyright©1984 by Morris-Young, Daniel
ISBN 13: 978-1-5326-3291-4
Publication date 9/21/2017
Previously published by Our Sunday Visitor, Inc, 1984

Preface to the 2017 Reprint Edition

"Beatitude Saints" was written by a young Catholic father of four more than thirty years ago. In re-reading the text, that no-longer-so-young now grandfather-of-eight finds reasons to smile and to take stock.

Many of the questions about the Catholic faith I had then have been answered, or at least corralled. Others have faded into non-significance. Others persist.

More importantly, perhaps, is that in re-reading I am reminded of the intensity with which I enjoyed grappling with those questions—and how that intensity has ebbed and flowed over the years. There have been tragic times when anger with God neared rejection of the divine. There have been years of lukewarmness toward Jesus, his message, worship.

And there have been times when the faith brought needed comfort and inspiration.

Interestingly for me—now at age 70—a different kind of keenness for the faith is working its way back into my bones. I am much more patient with God. Translated: I am more willing to embrace what life brings as his will. The good. The bad. The confounding.

I try much harder to just shut up and listen.

The best thing that this re-publication can do, it seems to me, is acquaint a younger audience with incredibly holy people of recent generations—Oscar Romero, Tom Dooley, Solanus Casey, Dorothy Day, John LaFarge, Maximillian Kolbe, Thomas Merton, Bernard Topel.

One update: Bishop Bernard J. Topel died on Oct. 22, 1986, two years after "Beatitude Saints" was first published.

Table of Contents

PREFACE TO THE 2017 REPRINT EDITION ... iii

INTRODUCTION ... 1

CHAPTER 1 ... 5
DYING OF SELF TO BECOME SELF
St. Catherine of Siena / Bishop Bernard Topel

CHAPTER 2 ... 17
THE GENTLEST OF MEN
Father Solanus, O.F.M. Cap. / St. Francis of Assisi

CHAPTER 3 ... 27
COURAGEOUS COMFORTERS
St. Elizabeth of Hungary / Dr. Tom Dooley

CHAPTER 4 ... 41
THE RIGHTEOUS WOMEN
St. Thérèse of Lisieux / Dorothy Day

CHAPTER 5 ... 51
THE BROTHERS OF MERCY
St. Peter Claver / Father John LaFarge

CHAPTER 6 ... 63
THE HOPEFUL FAILURES
St. Joan of Arc / St. Maximilian Kolbe

CHAPTER 7 ... 73
THE PASSIONATE SEARCHERS
St. Augustine / Thomas Merton

CHAPTER 8 ... 85
THE PERSECUTED
St. Thomas More / Archbishop Oscar Romero

Introduction

PLEASE understand that many of us who are converts tend to be a foolhardy, if good-hearted, lot. Few of us have had exposure to the Roman Catholic Church's teaching and tradition on saints, sainthood and saintliness. The same is true for the Church's emphasis on the Beatitudes and the spirituality of that backup team for the Ten Commandments. So you will hopefully forgive this convert's lack of inhibition in being presumptuous enough to launch a commentary of sorts on both.

This book cannot accurately be described as a collection of holy persons' biographies, nor anything approaching a weighty treatment of the Beatitudes. It is simply selective sketches of 16 deeply spiritual Catholics' lives grouped in eight pairs and wrapped in barber pole-fashion around a Beatitude. It is also a forum for some of my questions, frustrations, confusions and observations about my Catholic faith and practice of it. And I seem to have a lot of them: accurately discerning God's will, the role of Mary, authority, prayer, priesthood, ecclesial politics, sin — to list a few. Researching and writing the following pages have been an incredible grace in dealing with some of them. Yet I must admit I have emerged as simultaneously confounded and comforted by this Catholic Faith as I was the day I said "I do" to it at the age of 23.

There have been some surprises. Despite the fact I have worked as a "professional Catholic" in the diocesan press for the last decade and a half, I was increasingly impressed with the profound role religious orders have played in the spiritual formation of the Church. The amount these orders — their members and spiritualities — have contributed to who we are as a faith community today truly came home to me. You simply cannot explore saintliness in the Church's modern or distant past without stumbling all over Franciscans, Jesuits, Dominicans, and others.

The extraordinary role Mary has played and plays in this Church made a fresh impact on me. I hope I am not overstating the reality by observing that most of us who grew up as Protestants (nominal or devout) received very little exposure to Mary or the Holy Family as part of our religious education. On the contrary, there was an implicit and at times explicit warning to be on the lookout for putting any other before God/Jesus. And rightly so, eh? One of the concerns I had during the time before my own "rebaptism" and Confirmation centered on this. By becoming a Catholic was I somehow also joining this Marian cult business? If you have had conversations with fundamentalists whose neck veins begin to bulge when the veneration of Mary is mentioned, you know the general milieu that formed my prejudices about Mariology. Fortunately, I was assured by Msgr. John Donnelly (the editor of the *Inland Register* in Spokane, Washington, who gently answered wave after wave of arm-waving questions and accusations about this Church of Rome from his cub reporter) that Jesus Christ and His Father, not Mary, were the focal point of the Roman Catholic Church's worship — and even that the Vatican II Church was politely cautioning Marian devotees to double-check their faith-lives to make sure of this. That made me feel better and gave me the armor I needed and have used countless times since then in deflecting non-Catholic attacks against Catholic "worship" of Mary.

That said, however, I have remained uneasy about how firm a line is really drawn at times between proper recognition of Mary (role model, intercessor, etc.) and out-and-out deification of her. I'm not sure if I have come through work on this book supported or censured by the characters in it on this score. Almost to the person they displayed strong devotion to Mary, and yet they would be the first to stress the Lordship of Jesus. St. Maximilian Kolbe's entire ministry centered on Mary, and yet he wrote to his followers: "Please tell the dear brothers that they should never be concerned that they might love the Immaculata too much, for we will never love her as much as Jesus. And after all, the imitation of Christ is the source of all our holiness."

There have been frustrations. Even giving the Church as much of the benefit of the doubt as possible, I have had a heck of a time finding a satisfying apologia for the excessive asceticism some of our earlier saints inflicted upon themselves. I could understand if they suffered gallantly from outside abuse, but they actually rejoiced at what seem to be fanatic self-torments — physical and mental. I am hard pressed to find a model for this in Jesus' own life. While He might have been indifferent to His own comfort, He did not seem to go out of His way to desecrate His body. Is it paradox or hypocrisy that the Church underscores the rightness, even the sacredness, of natural law and then bestows its highest honor — sainthood — on persons who seem to have violated it in treatment of their own selves? For myself, I came into this book expecting hypocrisy, but have emerged favoring paradox. I no longer shake my head in wonder quite so readily when someone suggests a connection between a hair shirt

(I'd love to see one) and holiness. I just don't fully understand it. About the least offensive argument in defense of what looks at times like pathological piety is that it is a mistake to try to measure holiness with humanistic standards.

There have been insights. Working through this manuscript has opened my eyes a little wider to the saintliness all around me. I encounter it daily — on the street, over a beer, at work, on the phone, in letters. I was also struck by the fact that every saint seems to embody to at least some degree every Beatitude.

Perhaps you will question my judgment in linking certain people to a certain Beatitude. I don't blame you.

What has become most clear to me is that there are persons around us and before us — some officially canonized and some not — who have grown to be able to respond to God's will in ways most of us will never approach. To many, God is a combination of awesome mystery, logical conclusion, ultimate source, prime creator, distant father-power. To the saint, He is friend, confidant, lover. Most of us *listen* for God. The saints *hear* God.

1

Dying of self to become self

How blest are the poor in spirit: the reign of God is theirs (Matt. 5:3, The New American Bible)

Happy are the poor in spirit; theirs is the kingdom of heaven (Matt. 5:3, The Jerusalem Bible)

Blessed are the poor in spirit, for theirs is the kingdom of heaven (Matt. 5:3, King James Version)

BETWEEN the bishop's reception area and his main office was a small drawing room. Bookshelves filled with aging volumes lined the walls. If I remember correctly, the shelves also housed a few framed photographs —  one of the bishop with Pope Pius XII and another of him with some fellow Northwest bishops walking the steps of St. Peter's in Rome during the Second Vatican Council. The carpet was a faded purple. There were two simple wooden chairs, the kind your fourth grade teacher had.

I was interviewing Bishop Bernard J. Topel of Spokane, Washington, in that room when the Angelus bell rang across the street at Our Lady of Lourdes Cathedral. The bishop stopped mid-sentence, dropped to his knees, and recited the Angelus. I sat awkwardly in my chair, not having the slightest idea of what he was doing. When he had finished, he returned to his chair and asked why I had not joined him. I told him I would have been happy to, if I had had any idea of what he was doing. I reminded him that I was a recent convert — one that he himself and rebaptized (conditionally, of course) and confirmed, and that many of the Church's devotional practices remained as unusual and quaint (my Lutheran relatives had stronger words) as before that happy event. That did not stop him from insisting there was little excuse for my not advancing my religious education. He took a small book of prayers from the shelf, handed it to me, and instructed me to memorize the Angelus by the next day. I did.

Prayer, above and beyond all else, was a part of this man's life. So much so, that he wrote an open letter to his seminarians in 1974 exhorting them to lives of prayer. As a matter of fact, he told them to develop healthy prayer lives or pack their bags and seek different vocations. The impact of that clear and uncompromising instruction (thousands were reprinted and distributed and it is not uncommon to hear reference to it yet) came fresh to mind as I read about St. Catherine of Siena's reliance on prayer and her understanding of what prayer is. Her insistence on our being diligent in prayer and her distinguishing between what she called vocal and interior prayer was remarkably similar to Bishop Topel's distinctions between fixed, devotional prayer and what he called "mental prayer." Like the Italian mystic, Bishop Topel preferred the latter. He felt it opened real communication with the Divine, especially if we can cut down on our own mental chattiness and leave ourselves receptive to God's communication with us — even His silence.

Prayer — communicating, speaking, listening, sensing God — gave Catherine and Bishop Topel the desire and strength to attempt to strip themselves of attachment to temporal comfort. And prayer sustained them in leading lives that truly enflesh what poverty of spirit must mean.

Matthew tells us that Jesus listed poverty of spirit as the first Beatitude, and I would like to take an exception to the "rule" of this book by using one living spiritual teacher for reflection on this beatitude. All the saints and saintly in the following chapters are dead. At this writing, Bishop Topel resides at St. Joseph Care Center in Spokane, a man in broken health who has for some time been failing in mind and body. However, I probably would not be a practicing Catholic today if not for this humble tool of Christ; if not for being deeply affected by his poverty of spirit, or non-attachment to worldly goods.

Bishop Topel is undoubtedly remembered by most as the Catholic prelate who sold his episcopal mansion in 1968, giving the money to projects for the poor. He also sold his gem-studded crozier and jeweled episcopal ring, replacing them with a plain wooden shepherd's staff and a simple band. *Time* magazine, among other major news media, spread the story of this pauper priest. He lived in a $4,000 crackerbox of a house in a racially mixed neighborhood, solely on his Social Security check, eating what he grew in the weedy garden in his backyard or what people might give him. He put flesh on the demands of Gospel poverty — his own.

It is this Gospel poverty that first comes to mind when one mentions Bishop Topel, but I am convinced his public image rests on a more fundamental relationship he had with God, one in which his will was forged on the anvil of obedience and spiritual poverty. To be honest, if it was not for a glimpse of the holy through this man, I would have to reject outright as weird and flaky — even perverse and heretical — some of the lifestyles and "theology" of several saints, in particular Italy's patroness, Catherine.

If it were not for him, I don't think I would have had

the patience to try to understand Catherine's obvious hatred of her own body, her literal flesh-tearing scourging, her drinking pus from open infections of a woman she was nursing, her forcing herself to vomit with a feather, her eventual refusal to take nourishment, her invisible (to all but herself) stigmata and bridal ring from Christ. It would be much easier to admit that if people today said and did what some of our Church's saints did, they would be locked up and we would all throw away the key.

What does that have to do with "the poor in spirit" and Bishop Topel? "Father Bishop," as nearly all of us called him, was also flaky. There was the time I knew I was seeing my breath in front of my face one winter afternoon when I visited him at his little house in Spokane. He looked ludicrous sitting there in the middle of the tiny, sparse front room. He wore his hat, his overcoat, a tattered muffler and gloves. I wondered secretly if he was wearing the long johns a Jewish woman in New York had sent him. She had heard of his lifestyle, was deeply moved by it, and sent what seemed a rather practical gift. Bishop Topel kept the house hovering in the mid-40s during the winter to save on fuel. Since the poor had to, so would he. He lived that way, he said, because God wanted him to. It was that simple. Many mocked him; even those who loved him questioned the sense of it and saw the toll it was taking on his body. His diet was inconsistent, usually meager and rarely balanced. Yet this man was ultimately responsible for the operation of a multimillion-dollar organization, the Diocese of Spokane. He was in charge of the education and assignment of his priests and Religious; he was the spiritual leader of thousands of Catholics. What right did he have to abuse his health? Some even accused him of grandstanding, trying to milk the media for his own self-aggrandizement. Some Catholics were chagrined at what they perceived as a lack of dignity, decorum and responsibility in his actions. How could a man of his position live in a hovel, wear threadbare clothing, drive a decrepit car? These Catholics were also frustrated or miffed when he avoided their expensive fund-raising dinners. Who did he think he was?

I think it is fair to say he was a man so concerned about doing what he knew in his heart God wanted that he could take the criticism. His lifestyle of physical poverty was a source of strength for him and a source of witness for others. It spoke much louder than sermons on the obligations to not clutter our lives with things, our direction with busyness, our minds with trivia.

In him I came to see a paradox I truly do not fully understand. He redefined Church authority for me. His deep love of God, his singlehearted clarity, was authentic — so genuine and apparent to nearly everyone who met and talked to him, that you could not help but be drawn to him. Even persons who did not agree with him — and there were many on many issues — rarely doubted his holiness. And yet he would be the first to say he had little to do with the influence he exercised. He and I talked of this many times, usually in the early morning hours at the Chancery building where I worked on his diocesan newspaper. I enjoy the early morning, and Bishop Topel frequently arrived early also (some claim he was trying to escape the cold of his house). Thank goodness he did not make us keep the building as frigid as his house. Chewing on his tongue, as was his habit, he would stick his head in our office door and ask, "Aren't you going to make your bishop a cup of coffee?" Many times he would tell me in almost childlike manner how surprised he was at the impact he was making on so many people. Time and time again he would talk of God's love for us all and how desperately important it was that we come to understand the relationship between that love for us and our need to love and serve and listen to the poor. During one of those early morning conversations, I asked him why he never spoke at the National Conference of Catholic Bishops' meetings. "Don't you know what influence you have over them?" I asked, perhaps somewhat naïvely. "Don't you know how uncomfortable you make so many of them — with their palatial homes, priest-chauffeurs, domestic servants?" (Rather than stay at the luxury hotels that served as sites for the bishops' meetings, he stayed in a room at a nearby parish). He never really answered me directly, but only indicated that his place for influence really wasn't at those bishops' meetings. I never heard him criticize a fellow bishop.

The paradox I began to describe involves the kind of compelling authority exercised by this bishop. It was not secular or legal authority, nor ecclesiastical authority, but authority based on authenticity, and that authenticity and strength came precisely by this turning from seeing himself as anything other than a conduit of grace. Those scriptural passages about dying to self to become self (poverty of spirit) began to make sense for me in this man — as fallible and human as he was at times.

And it is precisely this emptying of self to make as much room as possible for the love of the Lord that resounds from the writing by and about Catherine of Siena. So many of the things that Bishop Topel said to me are echoed in what Catherine wrote and did. So when I find myself wondering if she were as much fruitcake as spiritual heroine, I remind myself of Bishop Topel's idiosyncrasies and his proof that the mind of God does not necessarily see things as we might. Suspended disbelief might best describe my reaction to her descriptions of her personal conversations with Mary, Jesus, St. Dominic, Mary Magdalene and St. Paul (among others). Yet I was reminded of Bishop Topel's admission that he saw the face of Christ come over the face of his own mother at the moment of her death. Perhaps only the poor in spirit can, ironically, become so bold as to have visions and speak with authority of things most of us would smile at politely and reject.

Please keep in mind that saints are a rather new language to many of us converts. This came home to me not long after I had been confirmed at age 23. Bishop Topel bumped into me as I was heading up the stairs by his office. I have forgotten how the conversation began, but from what seemed like nowhere he asked, "Do you know what you should want to be?" He answered his own question: "You should want to be a saint." That made about as much sense to me as saying I should want to sprout wings and fly. First, as I understood saints, it was rather presumptuous to think I *could* be one. At 23, I had enough trouble trying to drum up pure thoughts when an attractive girl walked by my car at crosswalks. How in the world was I supposed to insert saintliness into my thinking? Second, the world of saints seemed to belong to another time and mentality. I would have sooner expected to meet the tooth fairy on the bus than expect to become a saint. Harboring the thought of personal sainthood fell somewhere between presumptuousness and silliness.

Over the years my appreciation and reverence for the saints have grown (even if my ability to follow their examples has not). Yet this man issued a challenge and an invitation to me that no other Catholic or Christian had — a challenge that Catherine also flung at her followers as well as secular and religious leaders. When you have nothing to gain and are not seeking anything for yourself (poverty of spirit) your observations perhaps can be more bold and candid. I could not help but think of Bishop Topel as I re-read Catherine's encounter with a well-known Franciscan theologian and preacher of her time, Brother Gabriele of Volterra. Catherine's gentle yet piercing critique of his lifestyle contains for me two elements common to both her and Bishop Topel's poverty of spirit. In addition to pointing at the hypocrisy of his lifestyle, she invited him in a plain and straightforward way to make his life better, to bring it more into line with what he probably already knew God hoped of him.

Master Gabriele apparently lived in the style of a medieval prince. He had the walls between three cells of his monastery removed so he would have spacious quarters. His bed was curtained, his floor had luxurious carpets, his bookshelves contained expensive books. "How is it possible for you to understand anything of that which pertains to the kingdom of God?" Catherine charged him. "You who live only for the world and to be honored and esteemed by men! Your learning is of but little use to others and only harms yourself, for you seek the shell, not the core. For the sake of Jesus Christ Crucified, do not live on this wise any longer!" Sure enough, Brother Gabriele ordered his possessions sold and changed his lifestyle radically.

Somehow the poverty of spirit of both Bishop Topel and Catherine gave them the power to transcend the hypocrisy and cut through facades, protective sophistication and self-deception to the person behind them. Yet their exhortations to holiness were not so much aimed at hurting or humiliating, but firmly forcing a person to recognize the call to holiness he or she probably knew was there the entire time. In being invited to goodness by persons as good as a Catherine or a Bishop Topel, one is somehow empowered, encouraged, supported and given the clarity of thought and motivation to give it a try.

In a more generic way Bishop Topel exhorted the rich to recognize their preoccupation with possessions and to serve the poor; demanded those of middle income to reevaluate their second and third TV sets, expensive vacations and being "in style" every season; and asked the poor to not be afraid to offer up their powerlessness and prayers as sacrifice and not become bitter.

One of the fascinating things about the saints and saintly I have discovered, a little insight that surfaces when reading or researching their lives and times, is that they really don't say anything radically new, probably nothing that you or I have not heard during a Sunday sermon, read in Scripture or been taught in religion classes. One of Catherine's biographers, Johannes Jorgensen, distills the saint's teaching in a paragraph that could have also been written about Bishop Topel:

> "There are two kinds of love in man — the love of God and of his fellow, and the love of the world. There are two wills, the will of God and self-will. One of these two forces, love of the world, self-will, leads to interior unrest, sin, unhappiness, everything evil and everlasting loss. The other, love of God and one's neighbor, leads to interior peace, health of the soul, every virtue and everlasting life."

Why then, do we more clearly understand and more often respond to a Bishop Topel or Catherine — or a Mother Teresa or a Tom Dooley for that matter? The answer is a simple one, one that we all know. These people lived what they preached, they became as much a part of the message as the words themselves. They spoke to our hearts and souls, not just our intellect.

This is the effect, however. The cause is perhaps just as straightforward. Holy people develop personal relationships with Jesus, with the Father. The agony many of us might suffer is that we nod our heads to that truth and yet only partially understand it, only vaguely believe it. Our faith is near-faith. Our belief is half-belief. Our devotion is tentative, our prayer thinly disguised wishing. We find ourselves praying the prayer of the father of the possessed boy in St. Mark: "I do believe! Help my lack of trust!" And ironically in the saints and saintly we find inspiration and guidance but also run the risk of discovering that in being superhuman the saints have become inhuman. What do Catherine's constant periods of ecstasy, her hovering off the floor, her literal maceration of her own flesh have to do with the kids' carpool, spouse's mid-life crisis, or the overdue insurance premiums? It's fine for Bishop Topel to have driven an unsafe car, eschewed a telephone at his house, and undergone self-imposed malnutrition, but is that what God wants of me or you or our families?

Maybe it is here that we have come full circle and must sincerely seek to tap the poverty of spirit as embodied by a Bishop Topel and a Catherine of Siena. It seems it would be a profound mistake to make their message of love of God and neighbor more complicated than that. It would also be off base to think that their lives provide us with a mandated blueprint for our own lives. Bishop Topel said on a number of occasions that his lifestyle would not be appropriate for most — although his principle of simplicity stands as a constant exhortation. He even went a step further and pointed out that conversion to Gospel simplicity does not normally come like a flash of light. His own commitment came gradually and late in life. "If it took me a long time to grow, then it can take others a long time too," he said. "I don't get impatient and say that they have got to do it my way right now."

From a different perspective, Bishop Topel was saying that poverty of spirit is not the same as poverty of the pocketbook. This came home to me when I last visited him. I was scheduled to interview him for a magazine article on the subject of aging. I wanted to ask him what advice he had for older persons, especially those who were lonely, afraid and unsure. It was a painful interview for both of us. The bishop could no longer remember with consistency the faces or names of people, even those who were old friends. He would lose track of his thoughts and tire easily. Insights into aging, prayer, loneliness and death would well up behind his eyes, but his thoughts and sentences would trail off. More than once his eyes filled with tears. Lapses of memory, grasping for clarity, mental confusion were "all part of the suffering," he told me.

The strength of the interview could not be captured in the words he spoke, as powerful as they were at times. The man — Bishop Bernard J. Topel — was the message I walked away with. But more than that, I left his presence wanting to love God more.

Near the end of the interview, with his eyes focused beyond the room, Bishop Topel whispered: "I have given everything to God. If He wants my mind He can have that, too."

Blessed are the poor in spirit.

2

The gentlest of men

Blest are the lowly; they shall inherit the land (Matt. 5:5, The New American Bible)

Happy the gentle; they shall have the earth for their heritage (Matt. 5:4, The Jerusalem Bible)

Blessed are the meek; for they shall inherit the earth (Matt. 5:5, King James Version)

MEEK. Lowly. Gentle. The translators of Matthew's Gospel probably offer us more potential shading of meaning in their translations of the second Beatitude than in any of the others. "Meek' can connote a shying away from con‑   frontations, almost including a hint of cowardice in our current use of the word. And what does "lowly" mean? Economically and socially disenfranchised, oppressed? Humble? Contrite? Simple?

Gentle can bring us into a totally different realm. We can be gentle without being meek or lowly. We can be entirely powerful and yet gentle at the same time.

Yet surely the varied interpretations are views of the same truth, a truth perhaps better sought in the concrete than the abstract. Two Franciscans — St. Francis of Assisi himself and one of his 20th-century spiritual sons, Father Solanus Casey, O.F.M. Capuchin, provide incarnate translations who absorb any thesaurus-like debate over meek, gentle or lowly. They leave us with an appreciation for the difficult task Bible scholars must face when selecting one word to serve a kaleidoscope of potential meaning.

Francis (1182-1226) and Father Solanus (1870-1957) were pastorally gentle, heroically meek, and paradoxically lowly. Without trying to overstate the case, it is fair to say that my research and "alone time" with thoughts on Father Solanus began a change in my prayer life, perhaps even made me a little more humble. Yet it was studying the life, thought and spirituality of Francis that made Father Solanus take on even more significance.

To an incredible degree, Father Solanus Casey's life and ministry stand as a loud "Hah! I told you so!" from Francis. Although little is said about it by today's Franciscans, much tension existed in Francis' time about the direction his burgeoning order should take. A primary point of conflict was the training of the religious brothers. Francis, after much persistance, had succeeded in gaining Vatican permission for his new order to follow a rule of rigid evangelical poverty. To enter the order you had to give everything you owned to the poor. After that you would own nothing. Life was austere. Francis also insisted on an intellectual poverty. While he did not disrespect formal education and training, he eschewed an over-indulgence of it, for his brothers, for two fundamental reasons: first, to resist the temptation of book-learned wisdom becoming an impediment to true humility and wisdom; second, he firmly believed the brothers' lives of prayer and service were their living sermons, that lifestyle and example were the most eloquent homilies anyone could deliver. His order's charism would be service, not cleverness.

The story is told how one segment of the new order sought to have the group's rule rewritten, instituting one that would pay greater attention to formal study, such as that followed by the Dominicans. During a general chapter meeting, Francis is said to have pleaded in a loud voice:

> "My Brothers, my Brothers, the Lord called me to travel the paths of humility and simplicity and with me all those who want to follow and copy me. Do not then speak to me either of the Rule of St. Benedict or of St. Augustine or St. Bernard or of any other. For the Lord said to me that he wished me to be a fool and a simpleton, the like of which was never seen before, and that he wished to bring us on another road than that of wisdom. But God wants to put you all to shame with your wisdom and knowledge, and I expect that he will send his master of discipline and punish you, so that whether you will or not you must with shame turn back to your place."

As if by the great saint's intervention, Barney Casey from Superior, Wisconsin, showed up nearly seven centuries later with the same message — but spoken in example, appropriately enough, not words. Hampered by a lack of ability in foreign languages, especially the German that dominated his seminary training, Barney Casey barely achieved high enough academic scores to be ordained. When permission was finally granted for his ordination, it was to be as a simplex priest — a priest who can celebrate the Mass but, in his case, was not granted faculties to either preach formally or administer the Sacrament of Penance. Living in an era of ample vocations to the priesthood, his lack of priestly faculties made him almost more of a burden than a help, when assigned to a parish. He could not take a shift in the confessional, nor was it considered wise to send him on a sick call that might require hearing a confession. He could not deliver a Sunday homily, nor formally instruct on religion. As a result, the only duty his first pastor assigned him was that of sacristan, a job usually handled by a brother, not an ordained priest. His duties included making sure there was a sufficient supply of altar linens, that these were placed correctly on the altar, that altar breads and wine were provided for each Mass, that vestments were mended and clean, that altar boys were scheduled. He was also asked to see to the Altar Society, a group of women who met monthly and raised money for sanctuary needs.

Thus at age 34, Father Solanus Casey began a priestly ministry that you might describe as a clerical waterboy. How degrading this must have been. Deep down he must have known he had more to offer the Church than decorating the altar and providing a religious presence at Altar Society meetings. Anger and hurt, I am sure, would have been my reactions. I am confident that few of today's seminarians would accept this kind of treatment from their religious superiors.

Things did not get better quickly. It was not long before his duties also included that of being friary porter; that is, he answered the friary door and handled whatever business a caller might have — recording Mass offerings, taking messages for members of the parish staff, in general doing "gopher" work which so many parishes today assign to a volunteer or member of the youth group.

His lack of formal faculties and a sense of uselessness were a "humiliation and a cross" for him, writes his biographer James Patrick Derum. Whether he liked it or not, the Church "system" had made him lowly. Yet this "lowliness" brought forth in him a greatness and a holiness that might never have been realized in any other way. Over the ensuing years of his life, Father Solanus turned the humblest of positions — that of porter — into a ministry that touched literally tens of thousands of persons.

It is interesting to read syndicated columnist Coleman McCarthy's observation that "availability was at the core of St. Francis' poverty." So it was with Father Solanus. His availability, his charismatic simplicity, his willingness to listen, his sweetness, were what greeted those who came to the door of Sacred Heart Friary in Yonkers, New York. You might call it his meekness, lowliness and gentleness. It was these qualities that made so many turn to him for counsel and consolation rather than bother to seek help from others back in the friary. Yet anyone can be a nice guy, a willing listener. It was this simple priest's holiness that kept them coming back, that made his name spread among the faithful of Yonkers, Harlem, Detroit and Huntington, Indiana.

Ironically, he became a kind of burden for those with whom he lived. People wanted to see him and would wait in line to do so. The humble priest who was supposed to be answering the door was often too involved with people to do that, and Franciscans with "more important" duties would have to do it for him.

The special favors, the answered prayers, stories of unexplainable foreknowledge associated with Father Solanus could of themselves fill a book. Yet a simple truth undergirds every one of these anecdotes and testimonials to this simple man's holiness. He did not do anything special. He gave no particularly profound advice. He readily and easily deflected any praise directed at him toward God and His merciful Son. It was not Father Solanus' knowledge of canon law or of Latin conjugations that people sought. It was this priest's ability to help them move toward the holy, the divine. It was not an erudite and conceptualized religion Father Solanus taught, but one steeped in flesh-and-blood daily life. He was meek, and brazen unbelievers sought him. He was lowly, and the powerful asked for him. He was gentle, and the hard of heart listened to him. He helped all of them listen to God, to let God's Spirit work in their lives.

This tickled me because Father Solanus so clearly enfleshed the type of ministry advocated by Francis himself — an active one of example, presence and simplicity. I thought of the several Franciscans I know or have known, all of them fine men, fine priests, fine scholars. Still, I wondered how well they would survive the humiliations of Father Solanus; how many of them would give up their comfortable quarters, three squares a day, brandy after dinner, academic standing and social status. I wondered what Francis might have to say to them, this Francis who warned against "the wisdom of the world" and stated: "When the soul is troubled, lonely and darkened, then it turns easily to the outer comfort and to the empty enjoyments of the world."

As I rather smugly enjoyed this not-too-well-concealed personal indictment of so many modern-day Religious, I realized Father Solanus was chopping kindling with the log in my own eye. As I was relishing how well Francis and Father Solanus seemed to put the intellectually sophisticated in their place, it came to mind how I had felt about the devotional "style" of Father Solanus. In short, it seemed rather non-dimensional — in a word, blah. When someone would come to him for help, it was common practice for him to simply enroll them in the Seraphic Mass Association (a kind of third-string organization that raised money for Capuchin missions), sometimes for a specific intention, such as help for a sick child, or an unemployed husband. This action would aid the mission work, he told them, and include them in the benefits flowing from the mission Masses being offered wherever Capuchins served and noted prayers for their benefactors in the liturgy.

"Cornball," I said to myself. I have tended to dismiss this kind of devotion as a kind of "place-your-bet" superstition at best, "sleight-of-hand fund-raising" at worst.

What possible good could a priest mumbling "and our benefactors" thousands of miles away in another part of the world do for us? Really now! Why not just give a few bucks to the missions, know that God appreciates it, and let it go at that without this questionable bilking of the faithful (give us money and we'll rent you prayers)? "Can't people see through this kind of 'buy a miracle' stuff?" I asked myself, beginning to be pretty confident that the kind of people who are pursuing Father Solanus' beatification (officially begun in November 1982) are the same type who have pounded my desk over the years berating me for having "too much of this political stuff" in the Catholic newspaper and not devoting more space to the Blessed Mother and their parish carnival.

While we are on Mary, Father Solanus was also what a pastor-friend of mine calls a "Mary Freak." Father Solanus' confidence in the Blessed Mother's intercessory power seemed boundless, and he constantly implored her help for those who sought his. For some converts, of whom I am one, I don't have to explain the, at least initial, "so what" attitude we might have had toward the mother of Jesus. We have all heard, or might ourselves have asked, questions such as, "Surely she is due respect, but do we have to worship her? And worse yet, isn't this almost idolatry at times?" Not only did devotion to Mary by Father Solanus find little resonance in me; I was uncomfortable with the fact he seemed to be a formula prayer-reader. I could not find any convincing accounts of his phrasing prayer to God in his own words (not that he did not, as I am confident now he did). Why should this innocent thing bother me? To be honest, it fits into the whole "bead-rattling" mentality that many Protestants, and some Catholics as well, have about "formula religion." There is something non-thinking, non-participatory about this sort of worship, or at least that is the stereotype of it.

A good friend of mine, who is not Catholic, comes to mind when this salvation-by-routine discussion comes up. "I've got a neighbor who never misses Mass, apparently says the Rosary a lot, and tells me she makes the 6:00 a.m. Mass every morning of Lent," the friend relates. "But she all but spits venom at her own husband and kids, has lied about her neighbors, and thrives on gossip. She is downright condescending about my Lutheranism, and all but told me I was a hopeless case unless I partake of the 'sacrifice of the Mass.'"

My friend was not belittling the Mass, but was illustrating the confusion and even contempt that many hold for a Catholic worshipping community that is too often portrayed as one that depends on doing the prescribed thing at the prescribed time to literally earn salvation. Only functionary commitment seems required to win the grandest of prizes — eternal life.

Formula prayer is one of the things that harken up this whole prejudice for me, and it bothered me that Father Solanus seemed to fall back on it. I was coming to really like him. For one thing, his childhood, family life and life experiences were the kinds of things from which "Little House on the Prairie" episodes are made, and you just could not ignore the spiritual impact the man had on thousands, to say nothing of the only divinely explainable events associated with him.

For example, he was called to attend to a Sister Mary Joseph, who had been attacked by a severe streptococcus infection in her throat and was slipping into a coma with heavy choking spells. When he arrived, did he create a prayer unique to the situation? Nope. He took a book out of his pocket and started to slowly and quietly read formula prayers. While reading the Gospel account of the passion and death of Christ he would bless Sister Mary Joseph with a relic of the True Cross and place it to her lips and throat.

He kept this up for two hours. Not only did Sister Mary Joseph's choking stop almost immediately, it was not long before she had recovered and rejoined her community.

What I kept asking myself almost subconsciously was why he could not have forgone the recitation of holy-sounding syllables and gotten down to praying from the heart in his own words or thoughts. Why this pedantic, plodding, catechistic approach? It was so simple-minded, so unsophisticated.

And so lowly. Ahhh, the log in my own soul's eye. Not until cheering on Francis in his gentle struggle against those who would "upgrade" his brothers' religious education did my own hypocrisy begin to become apparent to me. The worldly criteria of trained and polished articulation of the faith, that Francis' own somewhat disgruntled brothers were trying to apply to their order, were not unlike the set of religiously chic hoops I had hoped the saintly Capuchin porter would have jumped through for me.

Francis and Father Solanus teach us that faith is not a mind game, and that worship begins in the heart and soul, not in our mouths. Father Solanus has helped me to attempt a challenging and sometimes profoundly moving approach to prayer that is new to me, but obviously centuries old for the Church. Father Solanus poured love, trust and hope into the prayers he would read or recite. Truly he did pray from the depths of his heart. I have come to learn that the definitions of the words are not nearly as important as the purity of love we can bring to them. The efficacy of formula prayer comes not so much from the offering we make of them to God, but from the extent to which they allow us to clear the soul's mind to receiving the grace and communication of our God. They can free us from concentration on our own thoughts so we can better focus on God. I will be the first to admit this is no great spiritual discovery. Yet, for me, it has been great. All of us are continually presented with new ideas, clever propositions, and compelling concepts. The presenters are many — media, work, friends, family, reading, school — even Church. My inclination is to give more credence to the shrewdest or most soundly argued ideas. My temptation is to apply the same criteria to faith, to my communication with God — or His with me. Francis and Father Solanus have helped me to peel back a few layers of this pharisaic wisdom and be more open to the wisdom of God and to the wisdom of those who are most obviously in touch with Him. And so often these latter are the poor, the lowly, the gentle and the meek — those over whom, quite frankly, I have educational and social "superiority" — at least by our culture's dominant standard of measure. Needless to say, I suspect God cares more about the state of my heart than the degrees on my wall, balance of my checkbook, or circle of friends. I wonder how my old Jesuit philosophy professor, who showed me seven ways to prove God's existence, would react if I told him a long-dead pious Capuchin had taken over as a coach in my fight to find a God that makes sense.

There is a good story about St. Francis' close friend, Brother Giles, that helps me much. In his old age, Brother Giles appeared before the newest general of the order, Brother Bonaventure. "Can one who is not book-learned love God as much as one who is?" Giles asked the future saint. "An old woman is in condition to love God more than a master in theology," replied Bonaventure. Brother Giles stood up, went to the garden wall and called out, "Hear this, all of you, an old woman who never has learned anything and cannot read, can love God more than Brother Bonaventure."

3
Courageous comforters

Blest too are the sorrowing; they shall be consoled. (Matt. 5:4, The New American Bible)

Happy those who mourn: they shall be comforted. (Matt. 5:5, The Jerusalem Bible)

Blessed are they that mourn: for they shall be comforted. (Matt. 5:4, King James Version)

THE picture that has always come to mind for me when mourning or sorrowing is mentioned is that of an individual or family grieving over the loss of a loved one. And when we read "Blessed are they that mourn: for they shall be comforted," it only seems right that God would comfort ("bless") someone who is suffering such a loss. At least at first it seems to make sense. But when you think about it, does that mean we "earn" this particular beatitudinal blessedness simply by following our human nature? It takes no act of will to mourn. Mourning is as normal as anger, fear or jealousy — and who is to say there might not even be a touch of self-pity in our seeing that door called death closing between us and someone dear?

Looking at the other seven Beatitudes, we can see that the state described by each cannot be achieved without spiritual action, not just emotional reaction. It seems to me St. Elizabeth of Hungary (1207-1231) and Dr. Tom Dooley (1927-1961) offer us lives that bring the concept of mourning or sorrowing into concert with this notion — that beatitudinal living comes at least as much from purposeful action as from accidents of grace.

Yet, it is more than reasonable to ask if it would be more appropriate to consider this saint and near-saint within the framework of the fifth beatitude (showing mercy). After all, both Tom Dooley and Elizabeth poured out their lives onto the poor — building hospitals, literally embracing the most wretched of peoples from lepers to the severely infected, sharing not just the surplus of their lives but the substance.

Like so many saints, including some chosen for this little book, Tom Dooley and Elizabeth seemed imbued with an innate drive toward ministry, especially in service of the poor. Both of these intense Christians accomplished a staggering amount of work in very short lives. By the time of her death at the age of 23, Elizabeth had borne four children (some accounts say three, but four seems more likely), been widowed, played a key role in a power struggle that included German princes and churchmen, founded homes and hospitals for the poor and diseased, and left the stamp of her kindness on Europe.

By the time he died the day after his 34th birthday, Tom Dooley had become a physician, served in the Navy, spearheaded the foundation of an international medical relief organization (MEDICO), written four powerful books, overseen establishment of seven hospitals in four Asian nations, and personally raised millions of dollars for his missionary medical work through countless appearances and lectures. It will be no surprise then to learn that Dooley kept an extraordinary pace and set standards for both the quality and quantity of his work which most of us would find self-destructive. But he seemed to derive strength and endurance from it. It was common for him to work well into the night, many of those hours spent answering some of the hundreds of letters of support and praise he received each month, even in remote areas of Laos. He set a goal of answering 10 letters per night when possible, at times jumping this quota to 14. This typically followed an arduous day of treating Laotian native tribes, performing surgeries, training local people in medicine, or working with his staff to carve a medical compound into the Asian jungle.

Why then focus on sorrowing rather than mercy? Dr. Tom Dooley (and, like a distant echo, St. Elizabeth) brought me to a fresh vision of what mourning and sorrowing can mean for the Christian. Slowly I came to see something Dooley lays in front of us with his work and his words, but in its simplicity can elude us. The sorrowing are not blessed by God as a reward for their suffering, but because through their endurance of pain and misery they come to an empathy and understanding of the fullness of humanness unavailable to others. They become members of what Dr. Albert Schweitzer called the Fellowship of Those Who Bear the Mark of Pain.

Who are these? ". . . the members are those who have learned by experience what physical pain and bodily anguish mean," writes Dooley in *The Edge of Tomorrow*. "These people all over the world are united by a secret bond. He who has been delivered from pain must not think he is now free, at liberty to continue his life and forget his sickness. He is a man whose eyes are opened. He now has a duty to help others in their battles with pain and anguish. He must help to bring others the deliverance which he himself knows."

It seems to me that this "deliverance" includes more than the gratitude for restored health or even the insight provided by seeing life in a new and special way after enduring pain and perhaps even near death. In Dooley's case, this conversion experience, if you will, sets him free from artificial convention, from slavery to the mundane, even in a very real sense from a fear of death itself. He seems to be a servant of little but the truth and what he sees as his life's work.

Both of these Catholics' "purposeful actions" involved direct as well as institutional efforts to minister to the sick. In other words, they were not afraid to get their hands dirty, yet saw Band-Aid approaches (if you'll forgive the word play) as only part of the solution. Still, it is their actual immersion in the lives of the medically and socially destitute that clearly undergirds their spiritualities — their mourning. One apocryphal story about the saint brings home the extent to which she was drawn to the poor and outcast. Elizabeth's mother-in-law, the Landgravine (like a countess) Sophia, was continually criticizing the excesses of Elizabeth's generosity, as well as her uncourtly manner. Apparently unable to convince her son of his wife's extravagance, Sophia thought she had the goods on Elizabeth one day when she found the leper Elias in the couple's bed, obviously put there for care by Elizabeth. Sophia dragged her son to his and Elizabeth's bedroom to show him how bonkers his wife really was, but rather than find the leper, Ludwig and his mother stood staring at Jesus Christ himself. After that, the legend goes on, Ludwig was convinced he was married to a saint.

The story parallels the legend of St. Francis of Assisi, who reportedly stopped along the roadside to kiss a leper. After traveling down the road just a bit farther, the saint turned around, but the leper had disappeared — the implication being that the leper was, of course, Jesus. This bears mentioning because Elizabeth eventually became a Franciscan tertiary (member of the Third Order), and biographers record that her reputation for service to the poor led St. Francis himself (1182-1226) to send his tattered cloak to her at the request of her friend Cardinal Ugolino, who later became Pope Gregory IX. It became her most treasured possession.

Elizabeth was the daughter of King Andrew of Hungary. In a dynastic deal characteristic of the period, she was pledged while still a toddler in future marriage to the son of the powerful German Landgrave Hermann I of Thuringia. To train her as a German princess and probably to lessen the lines of affection to her family, Elizabeth was sent to live and grow up at Landgrave Hermann's castle in Wartburg when she was four. Her future husband Ludwig (Louis IV) was nine at the time, and they were raised much as brother and sister, continuing to address each other frequently as brother or sister even after their marriage (Elizabeth was 14 when the marriage took place). This sibling as well as marital closeness probably explains Ludwig's consistent strength in resisting the Wartburg courtiers' discomfort with his wife, even pressure on him to send her back to Hungary rather than marry her. Reading between the lines, it is not too hard to see why the Thuringian upper crust had little use for Elizabeth. For one thing, she violated the niceties of court etiquette at times, like insisting on sitting near Ludwig at meals, a violation of local custom. To make matters worse, she would often only eat bread and water, particularly if she were suspicious the meat for that night's meal might have been gained illegally or in bad faith by a member of the court invoking Ludwig's name. The guilty saw this as self-righteousness, the innocent as scrupulosity. She must have been a thorn in their consciences, too, in her fidelity to Ludwig — and his to her — in a time when marriage was viewed at least as much a political tool as a sacred commitment. Extramarital relationships were as much a part of medieval court life as television is today.

With Ludwig's death during one of the Crusades, however, Elizabeth lost her protector and the years of stored up antagonism against her were let loose. Ludwig's brother, Heinrich, seized power in the name of the small rightful heir, Elizabeth's son Hermann. It is unclear if Elizabeth was made to feel so uncomfortable that she chose to leave Wartburg or if she was actually ejected with her children, but in either case she was pushed from her home. Word was out to Heinrich's friends that Elizabeth was not to be made welcome. She is said to have spent at least her first night in the bitter cold with her children in a shed where tools were stored and pigs were housed. Versions of what happened next vary from biography to biography, but it seems clear she was forced to give up her children, at least temporarily, so they would be better off, materially at least.

Elizabeth's mother was deceased, but she had a sister, the abbess of Kitsingen, who came to Elizabeth's rescue. Residing with her aunt, she was eventually reunited with her children. Interestingly, another relative, the bishop of Bamberg, who was the brother of Elizabeth's mother and the abbess, entered the picture and notified Elizabeth's father in Hungary of her troubles. It seems Elizabeth stood between her father and potential military chastisement by Duke Heinrich, because she knew this type of violence ultimately led to suffering for the poor. In the meantime, the bishop was busy in the political arena and apparently had sounded out German Emperor Frederick II about the possibility of proposing to Elizabeth, himself having become a recent widower. Legend has it that Elizabeth was so distraught at the idea of remarriage that she threatened to cut off her nose. While the anecdote seems a bit dubious, it is clear the future saint was firm against wedding again.

Some sort of reconciliation, or at least truce, was

reached with Duke Heinrich around the occasion of the return of Ludwig's remains and the funeral ceremonies. It was agreed that Heinrich would retain regency but acknowledge his nephew Hermann as landgrave, and he provided Elizabeth with dower rights. She was assigned the castle at Marburg and the town of Eisenach, where she had already established a hospital and two poorhouses. Elizabeth by this point had sworn herself to a life of absolute poverty, but now had resources with which to continue her work with the poor and sick.

As a sidenote, and not to defend Duke Heinrich's at times cowardly behavior, it might be fair to point out that erecting hospitals, leprosariums and poorhouses did not come cheap, even in medieval times. In addition, during Ludwig's absence on the Crusade, crop failures led to widespread hunger. To meet this need, Elizabeth authorized the pledging (mortgaging) of at least a couple castles and some small towns to raise the money to provide food. Given her already popular reputation as a spendthrift, it does not seem unlikely Heinrich might have been acting in what he felt was a responsible way to prevent the bankruptcy of the duchy. And he surely received encouragement, especially from his castle colleagues who felt someone who was building a hospital for lepers halfway up the mountain to the castle was misguided, if not dangerous. Even as Elizabeth's reputation as a living saint continued to grow, Heinrich maintained the private opinion she was insane. Saints do have a way of placing social order on a different plain of importance than most of us do.

Elizabeth's striving for holiness pre-dated her exposure to both the Franciscans and her eventual association with a spiritual director, Conrad of Marburg, who was commissary of the Holy Office in Germany. It seems important to point this out as there can be a tendency to focus on the last years of her short life — those spent under the severe tutorship of Conrad — as the ones during which her holiness was perfected to the level of saintliness. Technically this could be true, but to isolate those years and not see her life as a single whole might be unfair to her — and to us. I say this because it is a matter of record that very few married women have been canonized, and many of them were martyrs. It is hard to escape the empirical judgment that the Church reserves its highest honor for virgins. Is that bad? On the face of it, no. It only seems logical that persons who have pledged themselves to evangelical chastity for the pursuit of the holy might have a better chance of getting there than persons who do not. Yet, is there a danger in then seeing virginity as something holy in itself, or the corollary — seeing natural, normal, moral, sexually active lives as a step below, at best, or tainted with sin, at worst? I'm not trying to launch an attack on the Church's deference toward the virginal state, I am simply trying to establish that holiness — even saintly holiness — is a legitimate goal for all Christians, and perhaps to a lesser degree stick up for what I see as a tremendous lack of recognition for the deep holiness apparent in so many of those around us, most of them steeped in "ordinary" family life.

In the case of Elizabeth, this again seems important to note because it is interesting to wonder if she would have been declared a saint had she not been widowed. There is the temptation to see Elizabeth "escaping" her other life as a devoted wife and mother and servant of Christ to become a "true" saint through the mortifications brought her way by Master Conrad. Notes Theodore Maynard in his biographical commentary on St. Elizabeth: "He (Conrad) may not have been the only spiritual director of the time who came close to equating asceticism to physical suffering, but it would be hard to find one who was quite his counterpart. He knew that Elizabeth was already a saint, and he was trying to raise her to still greater heights of sanctity. Even so, one is shocked to hear that at least once he actually beat her with a cudgel because he thought she was not perfectly carrying out his instructions."

Almost like an agent or a coach, Conrad kept careful records of miracles and other events associated with Elizabeth. Was his motive to ensure her canonization, or recognition for his part in her spiritual development? As it turned out, after her death he was assassinated before he could complete preparation of Elizabeth's canonization case. His successor would finish the task. Although Conrad's death had slowed the process, Elizabeth was canonized just four years after her death in 1235.

It is fascinating that many of the miracles recorded almost immediately after Elizabeth's death — curing of the lame and blind, of paralytics and lepers — would be carried out by the miracle of 20th-century medicine and Dr. Tom Dooley's hands more than seven centuries later. Like Elizabeth, Tom Dooley was born to a well-to-do family (in St. Louis). After graduating from the University of Notre Dame and then the St. Louis University Medical School, Dooley served as a Navy doctor for two years, much of it on and off the shores of Indochina. It was there he began a love affair with the peoples of those nations that burned until his death from a virulent form of cancer.

If at a distance we can see how Elizabeth's spirituality was molded in the crucible of one-to-one care for the most destitute, we can almost touch the generation of Tom Dooley's sanctity in the same fire through the words he left behind. While Dooley wrote to expose his beloved America to the anguish of people in other parts of the world, his articles and letters and books reveal much about the man himself.

First and foremost a physician, Dooley was also a thoughtful philosopher, astute political observer, realistic student of human nature (including his own), street theologian, competent organizer and grand stylist of the English language. And he could play a mean piano. (One example of his ability to motivate others, to organize and to maintain sanity in a world that seems at times insane, is how he managed to have a zinc-plated piano donated and transported all the way to his jungle clinic in Laos, while at the same time not subtracting in the slightest from the resources of his work — providing medicines, training and care.)

Tom Dooley seemed to have a paradoxical approach to that work. On the one hand he invested himself totally and without apparent reservation in securing and distributing as much medical assistance as possible for primitive, oppressed and isolated people. A sense of urgency inflamed everything he did. Yet at the same time he did not expect the world to change overnight and did not see himself as the Christian physician-savior of these hurting people. We can see this in the advice he often gave Americans who expected his work to change Indochina into a wing of the Mayo Clinic: "In America doctors run 20th century hospitals. In Asia I run a 19th century hospital. Upon my departure the hospital may drop to the 18th century. This is fine, because previously the tribes in the high valleys lived, medically speaking, in the 15th century."

His down-to-earth approach was also apparent in the polite advice he offered persons with grandiose foreign policy ideas: "I feel we have to stop thinking of hydroelectric plants, dams, super highways and vast import-export programs. I think we should work more for objectives within the villagers' capabilities. We should find out what they want and help them to achieve this."

This realism can also be seen in the qualities he demanded (not expected, but demanded) in the people he chose to work with him in Asia. Describing the two men whom he selected to serve beside him in Muong Sing near the border with mainland China in northern Laos, he perhaps shared an insight into his own self-expectations: "They (Dwight Davis and Earl Rhine) possessed innumerable qualities that I wanted. They were not in any way religious fanatics and their idealism was balanced by a sense of realism, because in their overseas duties they had seen the stink and misery in which idealism must rub its nose. Yet they had enough youthful idealism to be willing to accept the challenge of any kind of job. They were in good health and had superb medical technician training."

Still, no matter how well-balanced with idealism and realism one might be, those qualities do not sufficiently describe, justify or explain how Tom Dooley could sustain the intensity of service he expended daily. And here for me lies a mystery. About the closest I can come to finding words to approach its perimeters is to quote a British writer of a half century ago, Arnold Lunn, who observed that "holiness is a force as real as electricity." Time and again in studying the lives of the saints and saintly we run into this phenomenon — a person able to seemingly ignore the laws of aging, of bodily demands, of mortality, if you will.

His Catholic Faith, his communion with God, was the source of energy that propelled him beyond the barriers of "secular" dedication. It is noteworthy that Tom Dooley was wary of "religious fanatics," for this jungle doctor was clearly a man of unusually deep faith. He saw the meaning of faith as much deeper than cudgeling others with guilt, fear or sales pitch. Despite the fact Dooley was highly educated and articulate, his faith appears to have been straightforward, uncomplicated. For example, he prayed the Rosary nightly. ("This Rosary meant a great deal to me," he wrote in *The Night They Burned the Mountain*. "It was impossible to taste fully the passing moments of our life. There was no time in Laos to pause; one had to keep running. But during the peaceful silence of night those few quiet moments with my rosary seemed to be the only time that I could get completely out of myself and be tranquil.")

His faith was something he lived, something that lived in him. It was not something to be intellectualized, dissected or "understood." To again borrow Lunn's words and apply them to Tom Dooley, St. Elizabeth and other saints: "To the ordinary Christian, God is a belief; to the saint, a lover."

Tom Dooley was aware of this loving God all around him — in the people he treated and in the beauty of creation. Reflecting on a journey he and his team took down the Nam Tha and Mekong rivers to make sick calls in remote villages, the medical missioner wrote:

"There were many things that vividly impressed themselves on my mind on this trip. One was an awareness of God, of the great pattern of the universe, the similarity of all the world, the magnificence of the dense green jungle, the majestic cathedral-like colors of the rain forest, the rapids and rivers flowing one into another. All of this cries of a Creator; this speaks of God.

"For me it is harder to know God in the tumult of plenty, in city traffic, in giant buildings, in cocktail bars, or riding in a car with a 'Body by Fisher'. But just as a manufacturer is stamped on American products, so is His stamp on all the universe.

"Here was God even in the decay of the villages, because in the death of yesterday there was a birth of tomorrow. We were lucky to be in the middle of this mystery and wretchedness." How do you reach this plateau, this state of holiness where being buried in the stench of misery and disease and crushed by the ungratefulness of ignorance and apathy do not kill your spirit, but somehow do provide the raw material of resurrection? Of joy? Of peace? Of contentment?

Dooley's insights are again straightforward: "I believe that poverty and malnutrition and wretchedness, which make health impossible, are not God-made, but wholly man-made, but the cure for the scourges, the compassion to want to cure . . . comes from God."

That's where Dooley found his desire to cure, and his vocational happiness came in serving the poorest of the poor. Yet he does not preach at us that the path he followed must be the same for us all. A much more fundamental Christian precept must first fill our hearts, he teaches: ". . . the only way man can achieve his own happiness is to strive for the happiness of others. This is a simple guide: every man has a responsibility to every other man." He simply states the gifts we are given are to be used for the service of others, and that in sharing others' pain we have taken the first step toward understanding the third Beatitude.

Maybe Dooley even gives us the basics for the second step. In his own way, Dooley admits that his total service to others became not a sacrifice but his greatest source of happiness. "This kind of medicine is my salvation, my hold on life. It is my means of expression. . . . I must treat patients with my own hands, reach out and give personal help every day. I feel that I must go out of my way to do it and to do it with tenderness."

Significantly, he wrote these words in description of the lucidity of life that came to him on learning the extent to which cancer had already invaded his body. It could not have been clearer than to a physician how imminent his death could be. He died about a year after those and the following words were written:

"I realized that I had become more aware of myself and my soul's adventure in the raw material of Asian life.

There was still much to do. I must continue to do this work as long as God allows me time on this earth to do it. I must continue to be tender, for to be tender one must be courageous. Now before my own highest mountain I must be braver than ever, even though bravery is sometimes a sad song. . . ."

Happy those who mourn; they shall be comforted.

4

The righteous women

Blest are they who hunger and thirst for holiness; they shall have their fill. (Matt. 5:6, The New American Bible)

Happy (are) those who hunger and thirst for what is right: they shall be satisfied. (Matt. 5:6, Jerusalem Bible).

Blessed are they which do hunger and thirst after righteousness: for they shall be filled. (Matt. 5:6, King James Version).

DOROTHY DAY always left me uneasy. My instincts said she was as cold and steely inside as she appeared in nearly every photo of her I have ever seen. My subjective and inarticulate assessment of her was that she was one of those stony-hearted liberals who basically hated everyone, especially those who don't share their world view. She appeared harsh, unfeeling, dispassionate, indifferent to human emotion. For me she belonged in that category of people who espouse love for the poor, but when faced with the smelly, ungracious world of the real poor, prefer to call a congressional representative or march in a picket line. (I was way off base.) It was easier to catalogue her as an idealogue than deal with the witness of her lifestyle and her exhortations to become the poor more than serve the poor.

Yet you also instinctively know that a cold fish does

41

not usually inspire the kind of following that she did (and does) without some real substance somewhere. Over the years, I have come into contact with a number of people in and close to the Catholic Worker Movement which she and Peter Maurin founded during the Depression. Most of them have impressed me as authentic types: a little surrealistic in the social and political realm for me at times, but committed, honest, sincere and willing to put their daily lives into what they believed.

So, I had to grudgingly admit that Dorothy Day would probably have to be credited with giving much more than just lip service to Church teaching on service to and advocacy for the poor, the hungry, the naked and the afflicted.

Given Dorothy Day's rather high-profile public life and well-documented outspokenness on social conditions and issues, she would seem more fitting for the beatitude on peacemaking, not hungering for holiness. And surely that would be justified. However, I discovered that Dorothy had written a biography on St. Thérèse of Lisieux — who lived her life hungering for the holy. What was this wide-eyed social crusader doing writing the life story of The Little Flower, who even Dorothy indicates probably knew little about social conditions?

When first introduced to Thérèse by a maternity nurse (and then again later by her confessor), Dorothy admits asking: "What kind of saint was this who felt that she had to practice heroic charity in eating what was put before her, in taking medicine, enduring cold and heat, restraint, enduring the society of mediocre souls?" The people championed by Dorothy Day — the street people — would have been grateful for any medical care; ate anxiously anything they could; had little choice about what they might have to endure; and were isolated by disease and poverty from nearly any kind of fraternal association.

Dorothy's life was immersed in the world of revolutionary ideas, causes and flamboyant, if not inspirational, personalities (from playwright Eugene O'Neill in the 1920s to the Cesar Chavezes and Daniel Berrigans of the present). What was she doing chronicling the life of a rather coddled daughter of a loving, two-parent family of comfortable means who seemed far removed from any awareness of the need for social reform? Keep in mind, too, that Thérèse entered the Carmelite convent at age 15. What could this child know or have to say to the apparent focus of Dorothy's life — the "people," namely the poor, oppressed, victimized? Dorothy herself admits saints such as Joan of Arc had held more immediate appeal to her. "Love of brother is to lay down one's life on the barricades, in revolt against the hunger and injustice in the world," she told her confessor after she had first read *The Story of a Soul*, Thérèse's autobiography.

I found myself pulled into a Dorothy Day I had not expected as I read her biography of Thérèse. I found Dorothy a mystic, a gentle lover of family, a loyal apostle of the Son of God, a pilgrim of deep piety. It became increasingly clear that if I were seeking insight into Dorothy's commitment to social action in her words about Thérèse, I had the cart before the horse. A little door opened in my mind: Dorothy Day found both resonance and sustenance in Thérèse Martin's single-minded pursuit of the loving God. What I found was a new look at Dorothy Day through the prism of her own words on The Little Flower.

Dorothy Day's empathy for Thérèse Martin's "ruthless search" for God undoubtedly formed the wellspring of her appreciation — even devotion — to The Little Flower. To be sure, at times it seemed as if Dorothy gently forced the saint through her own philosophical or even psychological filters. Maybe at times she read what she preferred into events in the saint's life or interpreted

Thérèse's words and actions with a healthy bias. For example, Dorothy made much of the fact that Thérèse spent the first 15 or so months of her life more the child of her peasant wet nurse, Rose, than of her own parents. (Thérèse's mother, Zélie, had given birth to six children before Thérèse and had been unable to nurse the last two or three.) Dorothy obviously enjoyed this fact. She wrote that young Thérèse's early infancy was lived in "a true peasant hut, made of stone and mud with a thatched roof, with a manure pile in the yard next door." Claiming the infant Thérèse would "reject anyone in a fine dress," Dorothy exclaimed, "She liked the smell of the poor!"

On different occasions and in different ways, Dorothy mentioned the Martin family commitment to serve the poor. "The Martins themselves did more than tithe," she wrote. "They administered to the poor, gave one day a week to their calls, and taught their children that it was a privilege to serve the unfortunate with their own hands, and do the works of mercy directly, instead of doling out advice and pious admonitions."

So, Dorothy Day was not put off by the Martin family's basically upper-middle-class status. On the contrary, she underscored that they worked hard for what they had, yet were willing to share.

This is important to note because Dorothy Day's own radical search for the truth of God very much includes the conviction that the poor can teach us lessons about God available nowhere else. "I've come to believe that precisely because she chose to live with the poor, day after day. She was able to see things clearly profoundly," says Peggy Scherer, who in a sense succeeded Dorothy at Maryhouse (the Catholic Workers' headquarters in New York City), and as editor of *Catholic Worker*, the movement's newspaper founded in 1933 by Dorothy. It would be of more than casual importance to Dorothy, it seems, that Thérèse Martin's credentials on concern for the poor be in order.

It is significant, however, that Dorothy clearly did not limit her working definition of poverty to one of economics. She seemed to deeply feel for the mentally and emotionally wounded of the world as well as those crushed by stark financial poverty. We begin to see what I have come to believe is a strong empathy for Thérèse on Dorothy's part when she described the saint's bouts as a child with what would have to be described in our day as mental illness. Dorothy suggested that "we should pray to Thérèse about those around us who are going through this suffering, these 'nervous breakdowns,' these delusions." To this day, Maryhouse (and perhaps others of some 50 Catholic Worker sites in the U.S.) provide hospice and care for the mentally ill.

Dorothy also reflected with a unique appreciation on Thérèse's lifestyle — a chosen one, a severe one, and not unlike Dorothy's own. "Her habit was of coarse serge, her stockings of rough muslin, and on her feet she wore rope sandals," Dorothy wrote. "Her bed was made of three planks, covered by a thin pad and one woolen blanket. There was a scarcity of food, inadequate bedding, no heat in the convent, except for one small stove in one room." Thérèse suffered in the Norman winters in her cold cell, and yet rejoiced in a severe life of hard work in silence that included six or seven hours of prayer every day.

Few biographers could be more authentic and understanding in calling these privations "spiritual works," "spiritual weapons to save souls," "penance for luxury when the destitute suffer," "a work to increase the sum total of love and peace in the world."

Here we have the heart of both Dorothy Day's and Thérèse Martin's passionate quests for what is right and good — prayer and penance, abandonment and acceptance. And here we have what for me is one of the most difficult aspects to grasp about these great women's spiritualities: how can self-inflicted suffering make the world a better place? How did St. Thérèse's offering up of little annoyances "increase the sum total of love and peace in the world?" Did Dorothy Day's adherence to a life of "precariousness" (the opposite of security) make her more open to the suffering of others — or did it lead to bitterness? I shook my head over and over again as I read Dorothy's accounts of Thérèse's various forms of suffering. At times there seemed to be an almost unhealthy penchant for pain. I can understand how penance as an atonement for sin serves to cleanse the soul and psyche. But I can describe only as mysterious or mystical both Dorothy's and Thérèse's literal need for suffering.

For example, not long before she died (when her incredible misery with the pain of tuberculous was most severe), Thérèse overheard one of the nuns attending her wish aloud that Thérèse could die to be out of her misery. "You ought not to say that," Thérèse told them, "because to suffer is exactly what pleases me in life." Another time she wrote, "My joy consists in being deprived of all joy here on earth."

Pleasure from pain? Holiness from hurt? Fulfillment from stripping oneself of even the slightest sense of satisfaction? Joy with its roots in misery and mortification? Listen to Thérèse's words when she was told the date of her "clothing" as a new member of the Carmel at Lisieux was postponed:

> "I suppose He found that the 9th (the day set for her clothing) delighted (me) too much. He wants (my soul) to have nothing to delight in. . . . And I know why — because He alone is delight in the full force of the word, and He wants to show his little ball (a term Thérèse used for herself at times) that it would be a mistake to look else-

where for a shadow of beauty. He who will soon be my Spouse is so good to me, so divinely lovable in His determination not to let me attach myself to any created thing. . . . Since I can find no created thing to content me, I will give all to Jesus, I will not give to a creature even an atom of my love; may Jesus grant me always to realize that He alone is perfect happiness, even when He seems absent!. . . . If Jesus does not give me consolation, He gives me a peace so great that it does me more good!"

Her deepest desire was to have no desire. Her deepest happiness was to seek no happiness. Misery, suffering, desolation were her roadmarkers for assurance she was on the road to holiness.

Thérèse did not stop, however, at trying to rid herself of just earthly pleasure. She strove just as mightily to remove herself from needing or seeking or taking comfort in the affection of others. She described how she fought off affection for the prioress, seeing it as a severe weakness. "I remember that when I was a postulant I had often such violent temptations to seek my own satisfaction and find some drops of joy," she wrote in her autobiography in a section addressed to Mother Marie de Gonzague, "that I was obliged to hurry past your cell and cling tight to the banisters to keep from retracing my steps. There came into my mind any number of permissions to ask, a thousand pretexts to give way to my nature and let it have what it craved. I can say truthfully that I gave up human love when it was at its strongest and tenderest because I had experienced the overwhelming conviction that I could not live any longer without God."

The paradox I find myself grappling with is that I am convinced of the depth of faith and even holiness of both Thérèse and Dorothy Day, and yet simultaneously find myself asking: is this really what God wants for us? Is natural, human affection a roadblock to righteousness? Is there not even a kind of implicit branding of Creation — both material and emotional — as patently evil in both Dorothy's and Thérèse's "theologies"?

I certainly have not come up with any totally satisfying answers for myself, but I did feel a twinge of spiritual relief (forgive me, Thérèse) when I asked myself: "Is this obession with detachment, suffering and near personal abuse the proper road to holiness?" and "*must* this be the road to holiness?" These two questions have ironically let me better appreciate the profound depth of penance and prayer as a road to the truth, as well as to let me off the hook (of not measuring up) by prying open a somewhat disguised issue: do we as Church and we as individual followers of Christ sometimes see this mysterious and awesome road to sanctification as the *best* route? Precisely because this kind of spirituality seems so remote from most of us, does it become therefore the most desirable? And if it is so desirable, why does God make it so difficult for most of us to understand, much less achieve?

Perhaps Dorothy Day and Thérèse with their radically different lifestyles, yet remarkably parallel spiritualities, provide us their own hints. While demanding of herself the most arduous of religious lives, Thérèse still emphasized that her "little way" is for everyone, that the real truth is love of God above and beyond all else. Her life energy became focused on God and mortification was the key. But listen to her description of mortification: "When I say mortification, I do not mean the sort of penance the saints undertake. I was not like those grand souls who practice all kinds of penances from childhood. My mortification consisted in checking my self-will, keeping back an impatient world, doing little things for those around me without their knowing it, and countless things like that."

Is it that simple? Just resist that second dessert, bite your tongue the next time an opinionated in-law tells you how to vote, and secretly clean the oven for your spouse and you are on your way to sainthood?

Who knows, just maybe. "It is the way of spiritual childhood," Thérèse said in response to a question about her "little way." "It is the path of total abandonment and confidence. I would show them the little method I found so perfectly successful and tell them there is but one thing to do on earth: to cast before Jesus the flowers of little sacrifices. That is what I have done and that is why I shall be so well received."

You cannot help but wonder to what degree Dorothy Day herself might have incorporated "the little way" into her own daily life. How many times did she invoke the French saint to withhold contempt when she might see a "prince of the Church" driven in luxury through the streets of a city where she knew hundreds of meals might be served for the cost of a limousine's tune-up? Did she thank Thérèse for helping her curb her tongue when idealistic youths found they could not "love" the guests of St. Joseph's, the Workers' hospitality house?

But what about Dorothy's lifestyle? Was it a form of fanatical Christianity that really cannot be lived? The Catholic Worker's Peggy Scherer provides an insight into that question in thoughts not unlike Dorothy's insistence that Thérèse was "for all," not just the radically zealous. Says Scherer:

"Her witness is a tremendous challenge, but not impossible to follow. And not distasteful, as you might think. People who knew her were inspired not just by her wisdom, but by how much she loved the life she lived."

And the reason she lived as she did was that she found it brought her closer to God. Truly Thérèse's and Dorothy Day's lifelong searches for truth and holiness converge here. "The total unimportance of anything in this world except God's love for us — this was the burden of her teaching," Dorothy Day wrote in crystalizing not only Thérèse's teaching, but undoubtedly her own life's direction.

5
The brothers of mercy

Blest are they who show mercy; mercy shall be theirs. (Matt. 5:7, The New American Bible)

Happy the merciful: they shall have mercy shown them. (Matt. 5:7, Jerusalem Bible).

Blessed are the merciful: for they shall obtain mercy. (Matt. 5:6, King James Version).

IN his book *Black Like Me*, the late John Howard Griffin (a white man who dyed his skin dark to appear black) told of going into a whites-only tavern in the South. Approaching the bar, he asked for a glass of water. The   kindly bartender went out of his way to give Griffin directions to a home in the area where the owners would allow him to drink from a water hose.

This anecdote came to mind as I researched and read St. Peter Claver (1580-1654) and this century's Father John LaFarge (1880-1963). Both were Jesuits and both dedicated much of their lives to serving and working with slaves and their descendants. Yet the visions they used in their work differed remarkably. John Howard Griffin's personal and powerful experience of the dichotomy between charity (he found it) and justice (he suffered its absence) illustrates well a basic difference in both of the Jesuits' work methods, and provides a case study of the

51

maturation of Church teaching on race and race relations during the three centuries separating the lives of the two men.

Known as the "Saint of the Slaves," Peter Claver was canonized for the extraordinary holiness (and appropriate miracles) he displayed during the 44 years he worked with the human beings bought and sold in the West Indies slave trade. Most of this time was spent at Cartagena, a key port of entry and staging area for the commerce in human bondage. It is hard to grasp the conditions under which the men and women kidnapped in Africa were transported to the New World, yet it is important to have an idea of the circumstances to better appreciate the person of Peter Claver. A ship's surgeon of the saint's era gave this testimony before a British Committee of Inquiry:

> "The men negroes, on being brought aboard ship, are immediately fastened together two by two, by handcuffs on their wrists, and by irons rivited to their legs. . . . They are frequently stowed so close as to admit of no other posture than lying on their sides. Neither will the height between decks . . . permit them the indulgence of an erect posture, especially where there are platforms, which is generally the case. These platforms are a kind of shelf, about eight or nine feet in breadth, extending from the side of the ship towards the centre. . . ."

The surgeon went on to describe the dank and cold holds, the lack of air and water, the sickness and disease, the neglect of boils and sores, the blood and mucus covering the decking and "shelves" on which the human cargo was forced to lay. The stench alone made it almost unbearable to even breathe the air of the slave holds. It was not uncommon for half or more of the captives to die or commit suicide before the ships reached their destination of the port at Cartagena.

In this day and age with its pampered sensibilities, it is hard to believe that Peter Claver rejoiced at news that a slave trader was about to make port. Armed with biscuits, brandy, tobacco and lemons, he would hurry to greet the slave ships as they arrived. After a visit with the slaves lucky enough to be on the open deck, he would descend to care for those below. Apparently the stench was often so nauseating that his interpreters let him make these sick calls alone. We are told that he considered this part of his apostolate to be of special importance.

It would be impossible to guess with how many dying men and women he somehow shared at least a fragment of Christian truth — and then administered baptism and perhaps last rites. His passion for the power and importance of the Sacrament of Baptism struck me as almost identical to that of Mother Teresa of Calcutta. Speaking to an audience of men and women Religious (I slipped in too) in the basement conference room of the Cathedral of St. Mary during a visit to San Francisco, Mother Teresa described how she and her nuns would gather dying people from the streets and sidewalks and tell them about Jesus Christ and His love for them — and then baptize them. With a divine twinkle in her eye, she humbly confessed that she was not positive if this procedure was totally theologically correct. For both Peter Claver and Mother Teresa, however, the centrality of baptism for salvation cannot be overstated. And surely it is an article of faith for Catholics that baptism is required for a person to enjoy the full beatific vision.

This brings up an interesting situation in regard to St. Peter Claver. While the saint abhored and fought the way the slaves were treated, he actually felt the slave traders had done an unintentional kindness for them by bringing them to a place where they could have the opportunity for baptism. No matter what abject torture and suffering they might have endured in passage, no matter what familial destruction might have taken place by tearing wife or child or father from the family unit, Peter Claver felt it was better to die a Christian at Cartagena than as a chieftan in Africa.

How should one consider that position? My first instinct has been to reject his theology as almost baptism by torture. Yet, his knowledge of baptism by desire was obviously not well-developed (that is, the desire to follow God's will, through grace, by those who have not been exposed to the Gospel of Christ or His Church, can become the equivalent of sacramental baptism). So, Peter Claver's zeal to bring salvation to others no matter the cost in human suffering in this world is defendable, even admirable. Yet how could he appear, to me at least, to be so narrow-minded and unfeeling as to see the act of baptizing and even catechetical instruction as legitimate byproducts of so cruel a system as slavery?

The answer is perhaps quite simple, if a little disconcerting, on the face of it. Peter Claver was interested in souls of slaves, not slavery. He did not question slavery as a social institution. Three centuries later and with much growth in Church teaching on social justice, we can judge the saint pretty harshly — and maybe a little unfairly. Perhaps it is also appropriate to point out that we hear little from Mother Teresa in our own day about the governmental, social and religious structures that, to phrase it politely, do not seem to be putting much of a dent in the number of diseased and dying reaching her door. The point, obviously, is that saint and social reformer need not be synonyms. Some of us have a nasty tendency of wanting to throw mud on the shining lives of others by seeing if they can be forced through the filters of unrelated criteria.

It is not unlike addressing Jesus: "So what if You *have* cured a few lepers and raised a few dead, the Romans are still here!"

On the other hand, what judgments could St. Peter Claver make on our modern-day American faith lives? Peter Claver lived the logic of Christianity. If we are followers of Christ, then we are dedicated to following God's will. And one of the clearest exhortations of Christ is to try to bring others to the saving embrace of the Father. My evangelical spirit is so weak I rarely break through social convention to *talk* about God, much less endure physical or mental stress to make His mercy more real for a neighbor, much less a stranger, and even less for someone who might smell and look repugnant. I am afraid Peter Claver might accurately accuse me of being an advocate of practical Christianity, while at the same time not giving much evidence of being one. This humble Jesuit would have all the right in the world to ask most of us if we find it easier to formulate schemes for interfering in or controlling our neighbors' lives than to love them.

He has certainly also earned the right to ask to what degree we have encased ourselves in painless Christianity, or have become worshippers of pleasure (even our painkillers are coated to be easier to swallow). It is tempting to write off the saint's mortifications (he slept three hours a night on the bare floor, scourged himself frequently, wore a hair shirt and rough wooden cross studded with sharp points, and ate little but small portions of fried potatoes) and apparent immunity to human stench and suffering as religious piety of another time, but it is not that easy. The man fought the same weaknesses as you and I. One day he was called to the home of a Cartagena businessman to minister to a slave who had become very ill. The slave was so ulcerous and infected that even Father Claver recoiled at the sight and smell. He became so upset with his lack of nerve and compassion that he went to another part of the house, flogged himself, and then returned to hear the man's confession. To prove his sorrow, the priest kissed the man's open sores and licked the most repulsive ones.

While the modern observer can point fingers at Peter Claver's apparent lack of interest in changing the social and economic structures that promoted and maintained slavery, he or she would be hard-pressed to find a Christian who better gave witness to the essential equality of all persons. And it is here on this foundational rock of God-given human dignity that the spiritualities of both Father Peter Claver and Father John LaFarge are built. Father LaFarge, however, was among those to work very hard to expand the work of mercy from acts of charity to acts of justice. Yet a case can be made that without the leaven of witness to the God-likeness of all, such as that provided by Father Claver, the eventual movement to the abolishment of slavery might not have taken place. In raw terms, Christianity forces whites and blacks, indeed all races, to recognize the dignity of all persons, and it raises the self-esteem one should have for one's own God-given body and soul.

Can we detect a similar process in Latin America today? Many who have spent time there argue persuasively that many of the so-called revolutionary movements in those countries have roots deep in the soil of Church teaching that all men and women are made in the image and likeness of God. This understanding of human creation has naturally enough led to the Church's insistence that adequate housing, education, health care and work are basic needs and rights of the citizens of this planet. That statement invariably makes the hair on the back of some anti-communist zealot's necks stand on end — and not without sincere, if misguided, reason. Totalitarians have clearly exploited the real needs of people by promising a better life, but delivering tyranny. Yet that does not change the fact that the Roman Catholic Church emphasizes the right of mankind and of the right of every individual to develop the natural gifts bestowed by God.

How will this teaching affect someone who has been subjected all his or her life to the whims of landowners, even if benevolent landowners? How will this affect you if you've watched your child die and come to realize that it did not have to be so?

I find the varying definitions of what is called liberation theology to be confusing, at best. Yet the essence of what is liberating about this religion called Christianity is the very fact we are the sons and daughters of the Lord our God and endowed with inalienable rights. The Church has always taught this, but the social implications have only gradually been felt over recent generations. The Church has moved and is still moving from a position of "accept this life as your lot because eternal life is the important thing" to an applied theology that views this life as part of the eternal one we are promised in the Gospels.

That is not to say Church people have not stressed the institutional nature mercy should also take. They have stressed it for centuries. For example, St. Vincent de Paul and his disciple Frederick Ozanam surely saw this. Yet the significant body of Church teaching on the subject has remained largely unused if not ignored.

Father LaFarge, in his autobiography *The Manner is Ordinary*, reflects on this in the context of the work he did in the Jesuits' predominantly poor and black missions of southern Maryland. "In preaching the Gospel week after week and month after month, one could always avoid over-obvious social conclusions of some of the discourses of our Lord Jesus Christ. Social reform was avoided in retreats and in mission sermons, and those who treated these matters were suspected of a certain degree of socialism."

While Father Peter Claver uncompromisingly gave his life to the spiritual and physical care of the slaves at Cartagena, his spiritual heir, Father LaFarge, insisted on adding the dimension of structural consideration. It is important "not only for remedial charity, but also for preventive charity, for such organizational methods, for such institutional improvements as would prevent the need of relief in later times," the priest would insist time and again.

"I wondered whether some of the hardest nuts of a social kind might not be cracked if we really took earnestly the Church's social teaching and applied it to the human relations I saw around me," he wrote.

It is risky business when talking about mercy, especially in this specific context of discussing two white men "conferring" mercy on blacks, that we do not become trapped by the notion of the powerful paternalistic ministering to the powerless. This has been at once the unfortunate and innocent bind in which the Church has too often found itself in its outreach to inner-city residents, often black, in this country. The "white Church" has had mixed success in bringing the message of Christ's hope to the hardcore inner city. Race is an important part of the picture, but so it seems is a nebulous mix of attitude, history and cultural reality that neither community can easily ignore. Parity of communication, mutual respect and understanding are the issues here, and are built more readily on shared experience than good intentions. Peter Claver and John LaFarge achieved this. Father Claver authentically suffered along with his parishioners. He gave living proof that the "imprint of the Cross is the only passport to the brotherhood of the unfortunate," in the words of biographer Arnold Lunn.

In less dramatic fashion, but no less authentic manner, Father John LaFarge also shared the lives of his parishioners in southern Maryland. After 15 years of pastoral work there, his future years as a writer and commentator on race relations, particularly during his more than 30 years at *America* magazine, the Jesuits' U.S. journal of thought, carried the earmarks of earned wisdom — experience, moderation, candor, fairness, open-mindedness, calm lucidity.

It was undoubtedly his credibility as a pastor of souls, as well as his clear thinking and courage, that undergirded his success in establishing many forums and opportunities for interracial dialogue, notably the Catholic Interracial Council in 1934. As repugnant as he found racial prejudice, it seems he favored the pastoral and practical approach rather than of arm-waving, foot-stomping displays of emotion. "The apostle of interracial justice among highly prejudiced fellow citizens resembles in many ways the missionary conversing with a foreign people bound by ancient tribal customs and taboos," he said. "Direct assault will not dislodge the fetishes. The idols will bow out only when people have become sufficiently enlightened to wish to remove them of themselves."

The gentle priest felt the same way about passing on the Catholic Faith. "Catholic truth can gain acceptance only by persuasion, not by bludgeoning. Respect for the inviolability of another's conscience is a prime requisite for all religious dialogue," he reasoned.

Fathers LaFarge and Claver both achieved that level of spiritual maturity where they preached without being preachy, pointed out sin without doing violence to the sinner, set the Gospel before us without insisting they be the primary interpreter. Father LaFarge's humility becomes silhouetted in an anecdote he tells about arriving as a novice at the Jesuit novitiate near Poughkeepsie, N.Y. He describes how he arrived somewhat late, but a brother was waiting for him to carry his baggage to his room and make sure he was comfortable. The next day Father LaFarge learned this humble "brother" was actually the novice master, Father George A. Pettit, S.J. The anecdote took on deeper significance for me in a conversation with a former colleague of Father LaFarge at *America*, Father Joseph Carroll, former business manager of the magazine. Father Carroll tells how as a young priest he arrived at Campion House in New York from the California Province to begin his work at *America*. As in Father LaFarge's story, a humble brother greeted him, carried his bags and showed him to his room. Father Carroll's "brother" turned out to be Father LaFarge, who at this point was a well-known and respected figure in American life.

Almost everyone affectionately called Father LaFarge "uncle," Father Carroll said, describing the priest as a unique combination of being "courageous, timid and foxy."

One cannot discuss Father LaFarge without at least alluding to his distinguished family, which dated on his father's side to Jean Frederic de la Farge, a refugee of revolutionary France who arrived in the U.S. about 1807. On his mother's side, he lists Benjamin Franklin as a great-great-grandfather and Commodore Matthew C. Perry as his great-grandfather. Several of the priest's eight brothers and sisters, as well as nieces and nephews, also became well-known. His father, also named John, was a famed author and artist whose murals and stained glass appear in many prominent buildings, including what many consider his masterpiece at the Church of the Ascension in New York City. Father LaFarge's childhood and adult friends read like a "Who's Who" in American and U.S. Catholic history. Theodore Roosevelt was a good friend of the family and influenced his vocation. He preached at the funeral Mass for Mother F.X. Cabrini, now a saint. His father's comrade and his own friend, novelist Henry Adams, spent much time with the family. Mother Katharine Drexel, Father LaFarge's "Philadelphia friend," helped him to establish schools in his southern Maryland parishes.

Despite the fact that Father John LaFarge was not born until his father was 45, and the fact his artist father spent much time removed from the family, it seems clear the senior LaFarge had great influence on his son, even if from a distance. It is interesting to note that in his own life's story, Father LaFarge chose to quote his father's notion of the Church's spiritual life being maintained not by the institutional Church, but "by anchorites in cells and lonely missionaries on far islands in the sea and by humble and devout people." (The description actually fits Father Peter Claver.) Father LaFarge also gave the impression that he felt the holiness of the Church was not safeguarded so much in chancery buildings as in the lives of ordinary and pious folk. His autobiography contains vignettes of several of the "Catholic parish saints" he came to know as a pastor, such as Miss Rose Nuttall. Miss Nuttall lived in a tiny cabin with her invalid father and mother. She did everything — cook, clean and tend to all their needs. "Yet every morning Rose would row two miles across the bay in her little skiff, tie it to the mooring post at the wharf and walk uphill two more miles to the church for Mass and Communion," Father LaFarge remembered.

It was this kind of living definition of mercy, of Christ-centered care Father LaFarge insisted should be translated into the civil rights and interracial movements. A student of the human situation and an astute observer of human psychology, he knew well that without concern for the individual (such as that embodied by Peter Claver), speaking of justice on a larger scale makes for a hollow sound.

Thus, it is fair to say that the kindly bartender who gave John Howard Griffin directions to a drink of water had taken the first step toward justice. And yet the power to provide justice was as close as the tap in front of him. Peter Claver and John LaFarge can prod us to look for institutional injustice invisible to us today.

6

The hopeful failures

Blest are the single-hearted for they shall see God. (Matt. 5:8, The New American Bible)

Happy the pure in heart: they shall see God. (Matt. 5:8, The Jerusalem Bible)

Blessed are the pure in heart: for they shall see God. (Matt. 5:8, King James Version)

WHEN the homilist says to us, "Blessed are the pure in heart," we tend to nod our heads and assume we know what is meant by "pure in heart." But just what does that tiny little phrase really mean? Does it mean no   bad thoughts dwell in our heads? Does it mean we always do God's will? Does it mean we have just come from confession resolved to never sin again — and in order to do that we are going to go home and lock ourselves in the closet?

To me, it has always seemed to be a non-thinking state in which nothing much at all exists in the heart/soul and mind, other than a feeling of exceptional joy or well-being. Being "pure in heart" always had a quality not unlike holding your breath. It was temporary, transient, illusive and tricky. It was like completing the winning pass in the big game, walking the entire length of a wooden fence without falling, balancing the checkbook on the first try.

63

"Purity of heart" has to do with those magic moments that strike our lives with joy, and then are gone almost before you have had the chance to truly savor them.

St. Maximilian Kolbe (1894-1941) and St. Joan of Arc (1412-1431) have given me a much more workable definition of the sixth Beatitude. Their lives provide a rich and durable texture for "purity of heart," one that has much to do with life as it is lived and people as they truly are, and yet does not lose the mystical aura that belongs with such a difficult notion.

Clearly, the inspirational life story of Father Maximilian Kolbe, O.F.M. Conv. (born Raymond Kolbe), is crystalized in the last heroic act of his life when he bartered his life in exchange for the life of a fellow prisoner at Auschwitz, the World War II prison camp whose name has become synonymous with hell. On a blazingly hot day in late July 1941, the Nazi SS guards were making rounds of the camp condemning men to death — in retribution for a prisoner who had escaped. When Franciszek Gajowniczek, a Polish soldier, was selected, he cried out: "My poor wife and children!" It was then Father Kolbe walked forward in his halting gait, hat in hand, and addressed the guard: "I am a Catholic priest. I want to die for that man; I am old; he has a wife and children." The names on the death list were changed, and the Polish sergeant's life was spared.

The Conventual Franciscan priest and the nine others selected with him did not die quickly at the hands of a firing squad, or even in a gas chamber. They died by starvation bit by bit, naked and cold on the cement floor of the Starvation Bunker, a prison camp innovation that was the pride of Auschwitz. Despite his age and ill health, Father Kolbe was one of four still alive after two weeks, and the only one reportedly fully conscious. The authorities became impatient and ordered that he be injected with phenol. He died on August 14, 1941, the Vigil of the Assumption.

This extraordinary act of courage is only the tip of the iceberg of a life lived "pure in heart." Even if you take his biographers with a grain of salt, one cannot help but wonder at the Christ-centeredness of this man's life. Like Joan of Arc's, Maximilian's life appears to have received divine direction from a very early age. Although it was kept a secret by his mother and only revealed after his death, young Raymond Kolbe apparently experienced an encounter with the Virgin Mary when he was 10. Praying before the altar dedicated to the Lord's Mother in his parish church of Zdunska Wola, Poland, the young Kolbe is said to have pleaded with the Virgin to know what kind of man he would become. Mary appeared to him offering two crowns — one white and the other red. The red, Mary said, represented martyrdom, the white purity. Asked to choose, he reportedly said, "I will take both."

Whether the child was being greedy, holy, silly, courageous, or whether his mother was sharing an apocryphal story, really does not matter. The matter of fact is that Father Maximilian Kolbe did lead a life of incredible sacrifice and dedication. His apparent clarity of life-direction and energy in pursuing his missionary work as a Conventual Franciscan (Friars Minor) almost leave you breathless. As soon as he had earned doctorates in both theology and philosophy and had been ordained a priest, he launched a movement among members of his order entitled the Militia Immaculatae (literally, the Troops of Mary Immaculate), and founded his first widely circulated newspaper along the way, *Rycerz Niepokalanej*, The Knights of the Immaculate.

This would be difficult enough for a healthy person, but Father Kolbe was frequently ill and at one time even suffered complete mental and physical exhaustion. As a result, he was sent to a sanatarium at Zakopane in the Tatra Mountains. He was treated for tuberculosis and, although around 1920 physicians gave him three months to live, he recovered and went on to expand and energize the movement for Mary that would eventually include hundreds of thousands of people around the world, including North America where it is known as The Knights of the Immaculata Movement.

Interestingly, the future saint gives us an insight into his own notion of holiness in his first issue of the *Knight*: "Everyone cannot become a genius, but the path of holiness is open to all. . . . It is untrue that the saints were not like us. They too experienced temptations, they fell and rose again; they experienced sorrow that weakened and paralyzed them with a sense of discouragement. . . ." Father Kolbe wrestled with sentiment himself, telling his companions frequently that they should resist becoming "sad and somber like hypocrites" but rather exude the joy Christ can build in a person's heart. One of those who labored with him on the newspaper in Poland, Brother Gabriel, noted the cheerfulness and sense of humor Father Kolbe consistently seemed to have, "often he laughed until the tears came to his eyes. . . ."

If Father Kolbe were ever paralyzed by sorrow or discouraged by events, he must have kept it pretty much to himself. For example, he was allowed to found a mission effort to Japan in 1930 and journeyed there with no resources save his cleverness, enthusiasm, confidence and four fellow Franciscans. Despite the fact they arrived with no money, no friends, and little if any knowledge of the Japanese language, two years later they had established a healthy friary and were publishing a national Catholic magazine in Japanese with a circulation of 60,000.

At the end of the fifth year, the band of five had grown to two dozen, a seminary had been opened and was nearing an enrollment of 20 Conventual Franciscan seminarians. The Franciscans' self-sacrifice and zeal were having a significant impact on many people of the country, especially around Nagasaki where the mission was based. (It is interesting to note that while Father Kolbe would not live to know the horror of the atomic bomb that would soon be exploded over Nagasaki helping to end World War II, the location he chose for his mission was shielded by its terrain from the bomb's devastation.)

Through much of Father Kolbe's activity one cannot help but discern an occasional sense of impatience. Not the kind of impatience you feel when a red light interrupts your mad rush somewhere, but the kind of satisfying impatience you feel by letting a five-year-old laboriously learn to tie his shoe despite the fact that you could do it in a fraction of the time. The priest's life seemed to surge onward almost as if by an inner voice crying: "There's only so much time for all this work I have to get done, so let's get on with it." And through all this, the man's sense of purpose and clarity of decision-making were remarkable. Only a phenomenal leader could have inspired the loyalty and service he seems to have inspired.

It is in the area of leadership, assuredness and almost undoubting confidence that Maximilian Kolbe and Joan of Arc have much in common. It is a legitimate position, biographies seem to imply, that for both saints this leadership quality could well be at least partially credited to the direct pipelines each apparently had to the Divine Mind. Father Kolbe's experiences of the supernatural or the divine or of providence (depending on your feeling about these kinds of interventions) were not limited to his youth. One anecdote hints that Mary let a rose petal flutter to his feet as a sign his mission in the Far East would be a success. In another, he confided to fellow Franciscans that he had a strong spiritual experience while in Japan that left him assured of heaven. It is unclear, but the strong indication is that he might have had another vision of Mary.

While Father Kolbe swore members of his community to secrecy after confiding in them about this, Joan was quite the opposite. She was very outspoken about the voices she said gave her guidance, particularly those of Saints Michael, Catherine and Margaret. Evidence exists to make a strong case for her actually having had contact with visions supplied from sources other than those of this world. For example, whatever private information she whispered in Prince Charles' ear, after passing a test by picking him out of the crowd at his castle, convinced him that she at least had strange powers. As a result, as we know, she then received a sword, a banner and command over the king's troops who were fighting in the Hundred Years' War. At first there was much opposition to her leadership by various army commanders and they did not want to obey her, but when they saw that success followed obeying her orders and disaster followed disobeying them, they cooperated and the tide of the losing battle with England was reversed. She liberated Orléans, defeated the British in four other battles and marched into Rheims where Charles VII was crowned King of France, with the "Maid of Orléans" standing at his side with sword and banner. Joan's mission to save France was ended, and she no longer spoke with the saints.

I am fond of the anecdote about the questioning she received by clerics at Poitiers who were more than slightly skeptical about her chatting with the saints. One asked if St. Michael had talked to her in French. She responded, with characteristic wit and forthrightness, that St. Michael had not only spoken to her in French, but with better enunciation than the priest's.

In addition to their senses of humor and deep convictions about their life missions, Maximilian and Joan have much more in common. Both were born of peasant stock, both came to be associated strongly with their homeland's Church life (Poland and France, respectively), both came to be cruelly martyred, and both took the world seriously.

What is such a big deal about taking the world seriously? Perhaps in the case of the more contemporary Father Kolbe, not much. However, for Joan of Arc it seems to this writer pointedly important. The spirituality of the Middle Ages and the pre-Reformation times had, almost without exception, much to do with otherworldliness, of detachment, of a severe asceticism. We need not look any further than some of the saints discussed in this volume for that to be clear. Yet here appears a young maiden who not only claimed to be receiving direction from various saints, but wanted to help Charles VII defend his kingdom from the English — on the battlefield, no less. How secular can you get? Even though Joan would carry out her mission in the most temporal of contexts, as a warrior there was no doubt in her mind that her work was pious — that of preventing her people from falling under political tyranny.

Some biographers try to make a case that Joan saved France for the Catholic Church. For one thing, they ask, why else would saints like Michael, Catherine and Margaret insert themselves into what would otherwise appear to be simply a dynastic quarrel? If the Valois Dynasty had collapsed into the English realm, then surely the forces that would bring the Protestant Reformation into full fury a century later, when Martin Luther's conscience and Henry VIII's libido changed the face of religion on the continent, would have engulfed France. However, that case smacks a little too much of triumphalism, at least for our day and age. We really do not have to go much beyond the sights and sounds and experiences of Joan's earlier years to find motive enough for her vigilance in trying to bring her country to peace. Exiles, wounded men, the destitute and other victims of the continuing wars paraded by her village.

Clearly, by helping to stabilize the political situation in France, Joan served her brothers and sisters as well as if she had founded a hospital. Still, if we are to accept this French woman's sainthood, we in a very real sense are asked to be at least sympathetic to her cause against the English. Should we be? To me it is an open question. Clues can be found, perhaps, not so much in a we-versus-they context, but by asking ourselves if we can or should remove God from the secular realms of politics, military, economics and the social order. If we do, are we actually despairing of His ability — or even right — to intercede, much less be victorious in these arenas? One of Joan's messages for us, it seems to me, is that God indeed has a rightful place in the deliberations and activities of the world. This is an important reminder in our own age when terrorism, the threat of nuclear holocaust, rampant amorality, incredible misery, hunger and poverty can at times make the world seem unredeemable.

There is a temptation to declare our "global village" a disaster area and retreat to islands of security, sort of spiritual bomb shelters where we limit the people, the books, the media, the exposure of life and reality as much as possible. These modern hermitages can go by names like suburbia, the club, the rectory, the campus, the study group. . . .

It is more than natural to want to retreat from hopelessness. Yet who could have been more hopeless than Father Kolbe after he was captured by the Germans and confined to a hellhole where human, much less Christian, characteristics were wrung out of you like water from a rag; or Joan after she was seized by the English, who would bend civil ecclesial and moral law any way they could to prove her a witch or a heretic. Yet, neither seems to have despaired under the most inhuman of circumstances.

It seems so simple and so obvious to now declare that both were able to exhibit such spiritual power because of their closeness to God. And surely that is true. But just what does this have to do with you and me? When was the last time you had a saint tell you how to handle an agonizing family problem? I know Mary did not float any petals to my feet when I was trying to figure out if our family should uproot and move to another part of the country. I am fully aware this might be sounding somewhere between sour grapes and irreverent, but I don't mean it that way. I must admit, though, I do carry a certain amount of jealousy for this kind of saint — or anyone who has God reach out and insert himself so clearly and plainly into their lives. I have honestly daydreamed during Mass about how wonderful it would be if suddenly a heavenly cloud were to form over the congregation, or over the altar, and Gabriel would appear — or even Mary herself. I've never figured out exactly what I'd want them to tell us, but somehow I know that just their showing up would make a big difference in my prayer life. Let me put it another way, and perhaps a little more to the point. Sometimes I just don't think it is fair that God makes himself so perfectly clear to others, and just leaves me hanging.

"You just don't listen well enough," you might say to me. "You must be more discerning and trustful." I agree.

Sour grapes and charges of divine favoritism aside, I do think Father Kolbe and Joan of Arc have taught me something I've never fully appreciated before. Like Jesus himself, perhaps, they were both charged by God to try — but not necessarily to succeed. This, to me, is a profound mystery, insight into humility and source of hope. And it has a lot to do with the lives we, at times reluctantly and at times passionately, try to align with what the Divine wants for us. We have all been commissioned (notice I avoid using "condemned") to lives of trying and not necessarily succeeding.

If we become parents, we will experience varying degrees of success and failure and sure heartache; if we become missioners, we will not only discover we cannot eradicate world poverty, but we are oftentimes not even liked by the people of God we are trying to help; if we throw ourselves into professed religious lives, we will be abused, non-affirmed, gossiped about and treated like cogs in a giant machine that tragically enough dares to call itself the Body of Christ. Yet here maybe the irony becomes less vicious in that when we think of Christ's body, it was indeed delivered up for failure. Deserted by most of His disciples and hanging in agony on the cross, Jesus Christ by most of our standards could have done a lot better.

Is that true? Was He a failure? Obviously not. The purity of heart shown us by Maximilian Kolbe and Joan of Arc allows us to focus more clearly on why. Both showed us by sacrificial example the power good has over evil, even as evil shows itself more powerfully. Both showed us the best kind of strength, a strength that is neither defiant nor yielding. And in the end both saints died in the knowledge that even in destruction, all is well.

7

The passionate searchers

Blest too the peacemakers; they shall be called sons of God (Matt. 5:9, The New American Bible)

Happy the peacemakers: they shall be called sons of God (Matt. 5:9, The Jerusalem Bible)

Blessed are the peacemakers; for they shall be called the children of God (Matt. 5:10, King James Version)

SAINT Augustine's and Father Thomas Merton's struggles with God were just that Neither's conversion was a neat and tidy little affair with all anxieties and weaknesses put to rest as a divine hand reached down   from heaven and patted them on the head as they said the magic words of acceptance. The journey to the Church was torment-filled, even wrenching, for both of them. I wondered if they had entered the Church much the same as I had, figuratively and psychologically crossing their fingers behind their backs, holding back a little something, keeping some unarticulated doubts stowed out of sight.

For me this early Church Father (354-430) and modern-day monk (1915-1968) provide special insights into the beatitude on peacemaking. Both were very much involved in seeking peace in the tumultuous social and religious times in which they lived. Augustine spent much of his "professional" Church career trying to keep the Christian world from tearing itself apart. He was frequently called upon to preside at Church synods and councils and was embroiled in the many controversies of the times.

Despite the fact that Thomas Merton spent nearly his entire adult life physically removed from the world in a small Trappist monastery in the Archdiocese of Louisville, Kentucky (Our Lady of Gethsemani), he played a significant role in the civil rights movements of the 1960s and later in the national agonizing over the Vietnam war and nuclear arms race. Few thinkers and writers were more influential in helping build spiritual and philosophical overviews of those issues.

Yet as historically important as both these men's contributions of thought and inspiration are in terms of civic and Church peace, they also have much to share with us on the level of seeking interior peace, and that is the focus of this chapter.

Oddly comforting for me is that both the saint and the monk seem to have taken a long route. And there can be a case made that perhaps neither ever reached a lasting state of tranquility, a permanent state of peace within their souls — at least in mortal life.

Biographers Cornelia and Irving Sussman attribute a quote to Merton as a nearly 20-year-old that carries great meaning for me. "Tom, you're an unpleasant sort of person — very," he is said to have muttered to himself. "I am vain, self-centered, dissolute, weak, irresolute, undisciplined, sensual, obscene and proud. I'm a mess!"

That quote really put me on memory lane, calling to mind an incident of ambiguous, yet real, significance for me as a 19-year-old freshman at Gonzaga University in Spokane, Washington, in 1967. I had chosen to attend the Jesuit-run institution because of the high reputation earned by its law school. The latent anti-Catholicism I carried as part of my Lutheran heritage found good grist for substantiation as I met my dorm mates, a good many of them Catholic preparatory school graduates, and the vast majority "cradle Catholics." I was amazed at their naïveté in a number of areas, especially in regard to women, alcohol and general worldliness. I shook my head as they shared tales about what they had been taught, convinced more than ever that this sect really did rule with repression, fear and an insidious kind of mind control. Ironically, however, as these friends began their late, if no less real, adolescent struggles, rejection and questioning of faith (like discovering they could miss Mass on Sunday and life would go on pretty much as it had before, unless their parents found out), I was beginning a confrontation with my own spiritual rootlessness.

Deep in my heart I knew myself to be undependable, self-centered, confused, and hoping to leap the tallest ambitions with the least possible effort. ("A mess.") A confirmed agnostic, I found the religious faith of others at times repugnant. A Gonzaga friend once asked me: "How can you not believe in God; in something more than just yourself?" I answered her with a question: "If I really believed that when I died I would have everlasting life and total peace and happiness for eternity, I surely would not be sitting around a classroom! That's pretty exciting stuff! Why aren't you out telling people about it? Do you really and truly believe in it? And if you do, why so nonchalant about it? It seems that you would want to share that kind of news with other people, especially if you are supposed to be loving them so much." By laying it on the line like that, I thought I was pretty hot stuff.

I really don't remember why, but one day I slipped into the side entrance of St. Aloysius Church at the edge of campus and took a seat in the side nave. I can clearly remember the rage I felt within myself as I looked up at the majestic crucified Christ hanging in the sanctuary. An impulse to stand up on that pew and scream an obscenity at that limp statue came over me. If there was really a God, why didn't He just show himself to me and forget this cat-and-mouse stuff? Why did He let the Catholic Church manipulate people's minds? Why couldn't things be more simple? Why was I so utterly unhappy?

Whether I stood up in that pew or not, I honestly don't remember. But I do remember reflecting later on the bitterness and helplessness and hate I felt in my heart. Then it suddenly dawned on me that if one hates, one must have something or someone to hate. I had taken a tiny step toward developing my own proof for God. If you hate Him, He must be there to hate.

Interestingly, Augustine was also a confused, anxious young man. He could have uttered youthful Thomas Merton's words of frustration with equal conviction. With no less vigor than Merton, young Aurelius Augustine pursued a life of "having a good time." Augustine fathered a child by one of his concubines and wrestled throughout much of his life with his own habits and desires. While somewhat fuzzy in terms of documentation, it also seems Thomas Merton unintentionally fathered a child during his collegiate years. Apparently Merton never saw his own son and, according to his friend Ed Rice, the girl and child were killed during an air raid over London in World War II. Other coincidences in the lives of Augustine and Thomas Merton are equally striking. Both were extraordinarily serious students, but voracious readers of all kinds of literature. Both men had a passion for the theater. Both men made and enjoyed friends easily. Both men loved to express their thoughts in writing. And both men struggled to control and understand their passions.

Merton biographer Monica Furlong makes much of Merton's fathering a child and apparently abandoning both him and his mother. She even suggests that much of his later motivation in life included an effort to atone for this. Was it guilt carried poorly or his actual previous lifestyle that led the Franciscans to change their minds about accepting him as a novice, after initially indicating they would? After being accepted on a preliminary basis, he felt the order should know everything about him, so Thomas Merton — even though he had been absolved through confession — made sure they did. After finding out about the "real" Thomas Merton, the Franciscans rather bluntly suggested he forget the notion that he was in any way cut out for the priesthood or the religious life. (Thank goodness he rebounded from the denial and persevered to later knock on the Trappists' door.)

So regardless of whether or not biographer Furlong overemphasized the role of guilt, it seems legitimate to ask if, in fact, Thomas Merton sought to join the Trappists solely out of love of God or to escape, to do penance, to construct a womb of rigid routine, to remove himself from worldly temptations, to hide in a place he assumed to be extraordinarily holy. Did he employ the same kind of logic to enter a religious community that so many have used in the past to justify entering marriage? An effort, of sorts, to remove oneself from the well-known occasion of sin?

Obviously, it would be tenuous and precarious to try to construct what the complex motivation — the hopes and needs — for Merton's Trappist beginnings might have been; however, it seems clear from his famous autobiography, *Seven Storey Mountain*, and other writings, that he was not going to be transformed rapidly into a different human being by association, by wearing a habit, by a prayer routine, or even by good will. The bruises of a life of sensual gratification had left their mark, and a life of prayer and chastity must have held a seduction of its own. Merton confessed in *Seven Storey Mountain*: "I had suffered so much tribulation and unrest on their account (gratification of the flesh) that I rejoiced in the prospect of peace, in a life protected from the heat and anguish of passion by the vow of chastity. . . . I imagined, in my stupid inexperience, the fight against concupiscence had already been won."

One of the key spiritual insights Merton provides us is that the follower of Christ is not exempt from the rigors or absurdities of life. He hints at this understanding in a reply to a woman who had written to him about her husband deserting her:

". . . I wonder if you are not doing what so many of us do: acting on the assumption that one ought not to be lonely and that one ought not to be traveling toward death; in fact that one ought not to be tempted to faithlessness and despair. This is unrealistic. It is also universal. But all of us Christians, since we know that we must live by faith and hope in Christ, assume that our formal commitment to Christ must be tested by its capacity to exempt us forever from any further anguish and danger of despair. But it does not do this. Quite the contrary. The Christian is one who knows that without the constant help of grace he cannot help but despair. And he knows that no amount of agitation and struggle on his own part can exempt him from this temptation. But once we have the gift of accepting our existential situation, everything is likely to come along with it."

The fulcrum upon which that letter rests, "accepting our existential situation," was used by Merton on the last day of his life in an address he delivered to fellow monks in Bangkok. It seems to provide the leverage for the many points he makes in that talk about monastic — and indeed, Christian — renewal. If you are like me, the word "existential" either sends you into grimaces or to the dictionary (and then into grimaces). However, Merton is talking about our everyday, undividedly unique and personal lives. No one has or will experience life and God precisely as you or I. Merton, through this uniqueness, this "existentialism," is inviting us to a come-as-you-are (not as you wish you were or hope you are or think you might become) look at life. The straightforward message he gave in that last talk is as potentially empowering as it is simple. Near the conclusion he summarizes:

". . . . If you once penetrate by detachment and purity of heart to the inner secret of the ground of your ordinary experience, you attain to a liberty that nobody can touch, that nobody can affect, that no political change of circumstances can do anything about. I admit this is a bit idealistic. . . . I am just saying that somewhere behind our monasticism . . . is the belief that this kind of freedom and tranquility is somehow attainable."

What does this have to do with us non-monks? Merton goes on to explain that the desire for monastic solitude is not unique to monks or hermits, but seems to "represent an instinct of the human heart, and it represents a charism given by God to man." This is extremely important for us, it seems, to believe and understand. We should not succumb to the temptation to believe that spiritual peace and tranquility are the reserve of professional holy people. Sure, we might be a bit preoccupied with the call from the principal that eldest son is flunking math, or the news that our flexible mortgage has been flexed. Most of us have at some time in the midst of personal crisis or familial chaos reached beyond the immediate circumstances and found a kind of sense of peace in the silliness of it all. I'm not entirely sure this is the exact sense of peace Merton is talking about, but I think it is close.

Appropriately enough, Merton alludes to Augustinian spirituality during this same last address when focusing on how one might move toward this spiritual calmness.

Again, the message is basic: move one's attention from self to God and others. Said Merton: "The simple formula, which was so popular in the West, was the Augustinian formula of translation of *cupiditas* into *caritas*, of self-centered love into an ongoing, other-centered love. In the process of this change the individual ego was seen to be illusory and dissolved itself, and in place of this self-centered ego came the Christian person, who was no longer just the individual but was Christ dwelling in each one. So, in each one of us the Christian person is one who is fully open to other persons, because ultimately all other persons are Christ."

Yet, again, how do we obtain this other-centeredness, this peace? Merton and Augustine show us two important elements. First is the acceptance of ourselves as we are — whether we are oversexed young men or middle-aged fogies wondering, "Is that all there is?" Merton's sense of humor well comes into play here and can give us the light of insight. Close friends say he was hilarious, and you can't help but sense a chuckle behind so much of his writing. Photos of him invariably seem to capture him on the verge of laughter. He appears to be telling us: "You just can't afford to take yourself too seriously."

Secondly, these men of deep prayer and experience show us that structure of some kind is important. Maybe we could call it ordered formation of our spiritual lives, or perhaps simply discipline. It can be argued that both men encased themselves in religious structures in coming to grips with themselves, not unlike prescribing spiritual casts and traction for fractured souls. What does this say to us? Most of us are not in a position to quit work, desert spouse and family, and join a strict religious community — even if at times that sounds enticing (my wife keeps threatening). One thing both Merton and Augustine teach us with their words and witness is that we have to pay attention to native calls for spiritual sustenance. For each of us, the response will undoubtedly be nuanced differently. Yet, not to respond simply puts off peace. And not to respond is perhaps a real form of selfishness, for if we are weak how can we better help others? Ignoring of self is not the opposite of selflessness. Merton teaches this well in his parable of the drowning person: "If you want to pull a drowning man out of the water, you have to have some support yourself. Supposing somebody is drowning, and you are standing on a rock — you can do it. Or supposing you can support yourself by swimming, you can do it. There is nothing to be gained by simply jumping into the water and drowning with him."

Augustine and Merton both chose institutionalization, if you'll forgive the double entendre, as the response to a need for channeling, for forming their spiritual seething. Depending on our walks of life, most of us have institutional, structured, organized options to assist us with spiritual formation — retreats, Cursillos, spiritual direction, prayer routines, etc. The irony in Merton, it seems to me, is that he clearly began to question, or at least call for consideration of, the role institutions should continue to play (imposed confines — physical, intellectual or both) once one has reached a certain level of religious maturity. Interestingly, especially in the light of his own history, Merton notes that the Cistercians of the 12th century speak of a kind of "monastic therapy," that the "period of monastic formation is a period of cure, of convalescence" and that after formal profession "one has passed through convalescence and is ready to begin to be educated in a new way — the education of the 'new man.'" For him, of course, this means the monastic life which has as its "whole purpose . . . to teach humankind to live by love." Yet he later points out that the essence of monastic life can no longer be described as "embedded in clothing, embedded even in a rule. It is concerned with this business of total inner transformation . . . (achieving) purity of heart."

Although Merton was speaking here of monasticism, his remarks seem as applicable to the institutional Church. What might he have had to say to us about our own relationship to this Church of Rome? In that last talk at Bangkok, the priest stressed to his fellow monks: "Remember this for the future: from now on, everybody stands on his own feet."

"This, I think, is what . . . Christianity is about, what monasticism is about — if you understand it in terms of grace. . . . (We) can no longer rely on being supported by structures that may be destroyed by a political power or a political force. You cannot rely on structures. The time for relying on structures has disappeared. They are good and they can help us, and we should do the best we can with them; but they may be taken away, and if everything is taken away, what do you do next?"

You "stand on your own feet."

Realistically, we in the United States do not have to worry about an imminent takeover of our churches by the government. But the question Merton poses can, nonetheless, take on real applications. If we have come to depend on the parish structure for stability, what happens if a new pastor comes in and (as canon law allows) dismantles everything the parish has established, such as youth groups, liturgy committees, school boards, etc.? Still, a wider application might deal not so much with concern about the disappearance of the institution but of the dissolving of the institution as the place one can continue to receive life-nourishing answers to fundamental questions of faith. How many times have older Catholics despaired of an institution that has "changed" since Vatican II and has put them into a position of not knowing where to turn? We have all, at one time or another, found ourselves, family or friends in these kinds of situations, and it seems to me that Merton's insights here would not be one of condemnation of institution but of acknowledging the limits of the institution and not being too afraid to "stand on your own feet," to seek the grace God promises us.

Merton seems to have become suspect of a tranquility that rests on institutions, or institutional formulas. And it is here that Merton parts company, to some degree, with Augustine, who very much became a part of the official Church, so much so that much of our tradition is footnoted by his thought and teaching. In a sense, you might say that the older Augustine became, the more he began to feel the need for rules and regulations to keep us on the journey toward holiness. In all due respect, however, I wondered at times if he might have been tempted to equate peace with an absence of perceivable conflict (at one point even justifying the use of force against heretics). On the other hand, Merton seemed to be moving toward a spirituality of inner peace based more on one's intimate dependence upon God and acknowledgement of self. The irony here is that Merton chose to remain with the Trappists — that is, within a system of rigid life-formula — and during a time of the Church's history when men and women in large numbers were choosing to cast off this form of religious life as oppressive, even damaging to the human spirit.

In a sense Augustine and Merton send us mixed messages, yet precisely because of this it is perhaps easier to understand them on the personal (existential?) level. It is not unlike the wisdom shared among alcoholics trying to stay on the wagon: you can't do it alone, but you have to do it by yourself. That seeming paradox has its parallel in both Merton and Augustine. Few of us will approach any kind of spiritual tranquility, even for short spurts, if we think we can push aside discipline, directedness, institutional "support." Yet these tools, these comforts, these religious crutches should not become ends in themselves. It should be admitted here that I am using the institutional Church, religious formation, the rules of religious orders and various pious disciplines as near synonyms — but of course they are not the same. However, in the sense that they all contribute to some degree in molding our hearts and minds and spirits, they are alike.

Alike, too, was an important part of Augustine's and Merton's blueprints for peace of soul. They shared their real lives, their real suffering, their real torment. They did not serve up myth and magic. For my money it is much easier to be inspired to greater strength by men and women who are not afraid to show us their tortured selves, their weak spots, their sinfulness. And frankly, in this regard, I have taken strength and solace from the fact neither of these men found overnight success in living out the pure moral life even after they had accepted Jesus as their Lord and Savior and the Church as their spiritual home. It took them years to bring conviction into line with actually living lives those convictions point to as best; years to break the bonds of habit and the slavery of sin. In a nutshell, we have a saint and a near-saint showing us that knowing what is right and wanting to be good are not the same things as doing right or being good. What I appreciate also is that even after their conversions and maturation into what most of us realize are saintly lives, the struggle still went on within them. And perhaps part of the essence of achieving peace of spirit is knowing that the struggle is worth it.

8

The persecuted

Blest are those persecuted for holiness' sake; the reign of God is theirs
(Matt. 5:10, The New American Bible)

Happy those who are persecuted in the cause of right: theirs is the kingdom of heaven (Matt. 5:10, The Jerusalem Bible)

Blessed are they which are persecuted for righteousness' sake: for theirs is the kingdom of heaven (Matt. 5:10, King James Version)

WHAT would you do if you answered your front door and the person there pointed a gun at you and told you to renounce any faith you might have in Jesus Christ or you'd be shot on the spot? Would you die rather than deny  your allegiance to God? In different ways, I have pondered that uncomfortable question throughout my life. Oh, I cannot say it has been an overriding issue that has kept me awake night after night, but it has popped up at significant times in various ways as, I suspect, it has for many persons. I can actually remember being certain of my strong faith at the age of six or seven and that I would be steadfast in that faith to the death, if necessary. I can foggily recall the dingy room of the little Baptist or Methodist (or was it Lutheran or Presbyterian?) church in suburban Portland, Oregon, where one day I assured my Summer Bible Camp teacher of my conviction. Later, during my "agnostic" teen years, the question was answered in non-

85

personal fashion: I saw the hypocrisy of the so-called Christian adults around me and knew in my acerbic adolescent heart that they surely would not even go to prison for Christ, much less die for Him. And if they would not go to the wall for their faith, what real value was it?

The question followed me — perhaps "haunted" would be a better word — into my late teens and early twenties, the conversion years. Without actually articulating it, I think I operated out of the assumption that if you could not confidently answer the "would I die for God?" question affirmatively, then you should not accept the obligations and glories that went along with declaring yourself a professed follower of Christ Crucified. The question forced itself upon me in ugly ways.

For example, would I let my need to be considered "one of the guys" numb my soul and mind during working hours to the non-value of locker-room or assembly-line conversation on the topics of sexuality, family, fidelity and honesty? This was really a concern of mine more than a few times during the days I operated a turret lathe for Boeing in Seattle. There is such comfort in being accepted as "one of the guys" in the locker-room context that we men (no sexism intended) can create a similar atmosphere just about anyplace. The obvious conclusion is that if I were to "apostatize" or renounce my faith in so light a challenge as to stick up for the Ten Commandments, surely I would crumble like a kicked clod of dirt if faced with anything approaching martyrdom.

In my early adult years, especially within a career as a kind of "professional Catholic," the apostasy question has cycled in and out of my life — sometimes in bitter fashion. When you are privy to what a good friend of mine calls the soft underbelly of the Church, it does not always look so holy, catholic or apostolic. Sometimes, I must admit, the humanity of us all has overwhelmed me and my judgments on "the Church" have been harsh. Rather than a refuge, a beacon or a course of strength, it has seemed to be a whirlpool of self-centeredness, mediocrity and hypocrisy. The assailant at my front door then points not a gun at me, but a mirror. And I wonder if it is apostasy to stay within the institutional Church, much less be employed by it as a de facto advocate.

People like St. Thomas More (February 7, 1477-June 6, 1535) and Archbishop Oscar Romero (August 15, 1917-March 24, 1980) have a way of shaking us loose from that kind of self-indulgent introspection and helping us re-focus on the beauty and courage that God can inspire in each and every one of us. They inspire us to raise our sights. Both men have forced me again to ask that question that has a way of shaking the lint off other questions of faith: would I die for my Faith? Would you?

Archbishop Romero's assassination on March 24, 1980, held more than passing interest for me. At the Oakland diocesan newspaper, we had for months been covering the strife in Central America, much of our news being generated through direct contact with missionaries, refugees, Church leaders and relief agency workers. The story we were gradually uncovering was dramatically at odds with what the U.S. State Department was saying. My reaction at Archbishop Romero's assassination, however, was somewhat impersonal at that point. Basically, I was surprised that forces opposed to the Church's human rights advocacy had grown so bold as to murder such a public and sympathetic figure as Archbishop Romero.

Archbishop Romero's death, or rather his life, came to touch me in a much more personal way within a few months. Word reached my office in early January 1981 that Msgr. Ricardo Urioste, vicar general of the Archdiocese of San Salvador, and one of Archbishop Romero's close associates, had slipped into the U.S. He came to

Oakland to visit old friends and to gain some respite from the extraordinary tension which had built up (in himself as well as the Church) in El Salvador in the wake of the assassination. With a little persuasion, I was able to arrange an interview with Msgr. Urioste at St. Therese Parish in Oakland where he was visiting with friends of long standing, Msgr. Michael Lucid and Msgr. J. Garcia Prieto. As it turned out, my wife Eileen and I also dined that evening with Msgr. Urioste and Father Joseph Carroll, a Jesuit who was working for the Diocese of Oakland.

I doubt Eileen or I will ever forget the time we spent with Msgr. Urioste. I remember being self-conscious about the affluence of both the rather plush St. Therese's rectory and the restaurant where we later dined. I could not help but wonder how long the money we would be spending on one dinner would support a campesino family in El Salvador. Msgr. Urioste, however, seemed non-judgmental about the economic disparity between the Bay Area and his country. He was a gentle, almost timid man. He did not seem the type to be running a tumultuous archdiocese, even for a short time. As we talked that evening over dinner in the quaint little restaurant, the faraway civil war in El Salvador seemed to come closer and closer. The tired faces, the horrified children, the running soldiers, the crying Salvadoran mothers in the news photos that regularly moved across my desk became less and less abstract — more and more human and real and alive. He told us of the women coming to him pleading for help in finding out what might have happened to sons or husbands taken from their homes in the middle of the night. He described the conditions that finally led men and women to risk death rather than continue to live with poverty, fear and degradation. Msgr. Urioste candidly admitted he deeply feared returning to San Salvador — but he would. He spoke of how Archbishop Romero had seemed to breathe strength, courage and hope into him and so many others, and of how he had suffered a great personal loss when the arcbishop had been murdered.

"It was easier to be strong when he was there. He gave us strength," the priest told us. Only later did we learn that Msgr. Urioste had played a pivotal role in the push-and-pull relationship between Archbishop Romero and those in the Vatican and his own bishops' conference who were uncomfortable with Archbishop Romero's defense of the poor and persecuted. For example, when Bishop Marco René Revelo was named auxiliary bishop of San Salvador he also insisted he be named the sole vicar general. Bishop Revelo was not popular among the clergy and had often questioned what he perceived as the Marxist orientation among some of them, as well as rural catechists, even declaring this at the Synod of Bishops meeting in Rome in October 1977. It later became clear that Bishop Revelo, despite a longstanding friendship with Archbishop Romero, had been appointed to the San Salvador See to maintain surveillance on Archbishop Romero for the Vatican and the papal nuncio, Archbishop Emmanuele Gerarda. Archbishop Romero stood his ground. He explained to Bishop Revelo that he was not about to fire Msgr. Urioste. He told his auxiliary kindly, "I harbor great hope that you and Msgr. Urioste are the two counselors and principal helps that I need right now as vicars general. You will also have your office here where I come every day so that every day, unless something prevents us, we can get together to plan and develop the work of the direction of the diocese."

Nearly all the factions in the Salvadoran conflict claim to be Catholics or come from Catholic roots. How, we asked Msgr. Urioste, could the well-to-do Catholics turn their backs on the violent situation, even brutal suppression, of their compatriots and co-religionists? Did the rich not see how they might be violating the Gospels? It seemed a painful question to him and we picked up by body English that one could not fully understand an answer to that unless one were immersed in the culture and history of El Salvador. Yet, he told us of how the powerful were blinded at times by a fear of losing their wealthy and their wealth; that this fear somehow translated into a hatred of communism. He spoke of how Church teaching on social justice simply did not touch these people's consciousness. For example, if their children were exposed to the teaching of social justice in schools, charges of Marxist sympathy could be expected.

I came away from that dinner with a picture of a Church in schism — no, actually a picture of two churches. One might be distinguished by an emphasis on religion as cultural trapping, a theology that underscores personal piety unrelated to flesh and blood; the other is enlivened by the question, "what would Jesus want me to do?" enriched by prayer and the challenge of bringing Jesus, food, clothing, medicine and solace to those hungering both spiritually and physically.

Eileen and I were subdued as we dropped Msgr. Urioste off at St. Therese's rectory that night. He asked us to pray for him — not in that "see you tomorrow" way, but from the heart. We really did not know how to say goodbye. How do you wish a "good evening" to someone who has just spent several hours sharing insights and fears about a cruel situation such as that facing him in El Salvador? How do you say good-night to someone who might be shot, butchered or tortured within days? Eileen hugged him awkwardly; I shook his hand.

We talked about El Salvador, its people and Msgr. Urioste late into the night. As we lay in bed, I told Eileen I thought I should travel to El Salvador and generate accurate stories about what was going on. I felt brave and afraid and invigorated. We discussed withholding our income tax in protest of U.S. policies and how that action could affect our lives — attachment of wages, jeopardizing employment, being stigmatized as radical or kooky During the ensuing days, weeks and months, however, that zealousness waned. Sure, I wrote some editorials questioning, even condemning, some of our nation's policies in Central America, but the fervor faded. Other things pushed into our newspaper's headlines: nuclear weapons, Poland, homosexuality, etc. Other things moved into our daily focus: a move to a new home, paying bills, scuba diving, the kids and school.

Yet, temporarily I had felt cleansed, in a sense, by the effect of actually asking myself: "Would I risk my life for these people; for the truth?" I had almost answered, "Yes!" But the zeal fizzled.

I was aware of the anguish of the Salvadoran people and did next to nothing about it. I mention this not to breast-beat, but to illustrate one of the many forms of persecution shared by the voiceless of Central America in general and by Archbishop Romero personally — apathy. It is one thing to have someone tell you to take a hike; it is another to have them care less if you hike or not. Returning to San Salvador from Rome in May 1979, Archbishop Romero remarked: "At times the insensibility of Europe to Latin America makes your heart ache more and makes one from Latin America in Europe feel like a missionary, like an awakener of conscience, of universal brotherhood, begging for understanding and love for our huge and complex problems in Latin America."

It seems that this apathy — not only of Europeans, but of North Americans and citizens of other parts of the world — is only one of the many forms of persecution suffered by Archbishop Romero. It is natural and understandable that we tend to immediately focus on his persecution by the Salvadoran government and its security forces, although they would deny vehemently any such thing. But his suffering must have been just as painful, perhaps more so, from other quarters — notably his fellow bishops as well as some Vatican officials, to say nothing of the country's papal representative, Archbishop Gerada.

Examples abound of the differences between Archbishop Romero and the nuncio, but one symbolizes them for me. Government troops had invaded the Salvadoran town of Aguilares and occupied the church for weeks, reportedly desecrating the Blessed Sacrament and killing the sexton and numerous parishioners. The government had deported four priests despite Archbishop Romero's strong protests. Investigations into the murders of other priests were all but ignored. Archbishop Romero protested all these events, demanding investigations and explanations. Little other than perfunctory responses came from the government.

It was within this context then that the Priests' Senate of the archdiocese voted 11-1 against Archbishop Romero attending the inauguration of the country's new president, General Carlos Humberto Romero (the name is coincidental). However, the nuncio and two Salvadoran bishops, who had close ties with the powerful, chose to attend. How could anyone draw any other conclusion than the pope's official representative tacitly endorsed the government, a government whose policies and security forces were repeatedly denounced by Archbishop Romero?

It is no surprise that "the file" on Archbishop Romero at the Vatican was rather negative. His dealing with various heads of congregations as well as other curial offices must have been agonizing, especially for one as singularly devoted to the central authority of the Church as Archbishop Romero. One cannot help but wonder if this subtle form of persecution was not all the more acute for the man. If he had been a radical or ultra-progressive, the disfavor of Rome might not have bothered him much. Yet he was very much a traditionalist. The irony is that his honesty in seeing the persecution of the campesinos for what it was, and speaking out against it, set him at odds with persons with whom he might very well have been more in tune philosophically and theologically than those who supported him.

For me, a clarity of understanding and unwillingness to dilute conviction draw Archbishop Romero and Thomas More together, despite the five centuries that separated their lives. Oscar Romero could have taken the easy road. He could have taken a half-step back on his unwavering insistence that the Church remain solidly behind its defense of the powerless and the persecuted. He could have maintained a level of public criticism of the authorities, the military, the rich and the vengeful radicals that would have appeared appropriate and sustain his credibility with the progressives, yet not be so pointed as to pierce the kindly facades hoisted by those who those who call torture truth, death defense and hatred conviction. He did not tone down his preaching, however (as the papal nuncio in Costa Rica had urged him to do not long before his assassination). He did not become militantly luke-warm, nor bend to ecclesiastical coercion.

He operated from that most traditional, bedrock principle that God will provide you the truth if you pray for it, and form your conscience carefully. You can feel this gentle strength in the conclusion to a letter to the papal nuncio (a letter explaining why he had carried through on an action displeasing to Archbishop Gerada) in which he concludes: "Finally, Your Excellency, I propose to you that we analyze and reflect serenely now, after the fact, on what has been done in accord with my conscience."

Like Thomas More, Oscar Romero knew that true allegiance to authority is not unquestioning, uncritical acceptance of everything that that authority might suggest. In the case of the English saint, it was ultimately this integrity that cost him his life. He simply would not deny what he knew to be true — that no lay authority could have jurisdiction over the Church of Christ. His assailant, King Henry VIII, stood at his door with a broadaxe and demanded he deny his Faith. Rather than take the Oath of Supremacy, which declared King Henry head of the Church, Thomas More went to his death.

As *A Man For All Seasons* dramatically leads us to do, we tend to focus on the climactic martyrdom of Thomas More's life. But do we then perhaps miss the soul of his persecution? As in the case of Archbishop Romero, Thomas More could have taken the respectable road out and saved his life. As a matter of fact, it would have been easy for him to rationalize this "soft apostasy." Thomas More was a man gifted with word and thought. If there was anyone in the kingdom who could have formulated an airtight rationale to cloak King Henry's lust and ambition in compelling language, it was Thomas More. Few men were more respected. Yet it was precisely the general respect properly owned by him that made his acceptance of the oath for King Henry critical. More was an international scholar, an eminent lawyer, former lord chancellor of England, former speaker in Parliament, high steward of Oxford, and one of the realm's most prominent of knighted citizens. Even Thomas More's silence on the issue was too loud a protest. Henry must have More's acquiescence. Henry failed. Thomas More was sentenced to death.

More's persecution went even deeper than facing the temptation to simply (if cleverly) cave in to Henry. Apparently, his own family did not entirely understand his conviction, nor wholly support it, because it did, in fact, represent his death. How hard it must have been to tell them he was choosing to be separated from them — to die and leave them — for a higher purpose: loyalty to God and Church. Henry and his minister, Thomas Cromwell, must have sensed the potential power of this "tool" too, because they forbade visits from family members during the latter part of the saint's imprisonment. Maybe it is because I am the father of four that this affects me so deeply. What an indescribable agony it would be to know that death will soon separate you from your family, and to also know that you could escape that cup if you just compromised on something so many others were accepting as pro forma civic duty. And yet what is fathering all about at its most profound levels if it is not providing living example? And when can example be more powerfully expressed than when it is most arduously difficult to remain true to the truth?

This will undoubtedly verge on sounding corny, but any meditations on the lives and examples of Thomas More and Archbishop Romero have helped me be just a little more brave — at least most of the time. I still don't know what I would do if someone pointed a gun at me and demanded I renounce Christ or die. But I do know I have made some spiritual baby steps toward trying to avoid turning my back on Him with white lies, uncritical acceptance of conventional amorality, and living my life as if my example to others (especially my children) did not make an important difference.

www.ingramcontent.com/pod-product-compliance
Lightning Source LLC
Chambersburg PA
CBHW070311100426
42743CB00011B/2434